A PORTRAIT OF THE
LANCASHIRE TEXTILE INDUSTRY

A Portrait of
THE LANCASHIRE
TEXTILE INDUSTRY

L. H. C. TIPPETT

London
OXFORD UNIVERSITY PRESS
NEW YORK   TORONTO
1969

Oxford University Press, Ely House, London W.1

GLASGOW NEW YORK TORONTO MELBOURNE WELLINGTON
CAPE TOWN SALISBURY IBADAN NAIROBI LUSAKA ADDIS ABABA
BOMBAY CALCUTTA MADRAS KARACHI LAHORE DACCA
KUALA LUMPUR HONG KONG SINGAPORE TOKYO

Printed in Great Britain by
The Camelot Press Ltd., London and Southampton

Contents

Illustrations

Preface

I entered the service of the (then) Lancashire cotton industry in 1925 by joining the staff of the Shirley Institute, the industry's research organization, and continued in that service for forty years. During that time I became interested in all sides of the industry: in the fibres it uses; the cloths it makes and what gives them their particular properties; the machines and processes and what they do to the fibres; the work of the operatives and the organization of that work into a factory system; management methods; the organization of mills into firms and into an industry; the many institutions of the industry; mill life and what the inside of the mill is like; the marketing arrangements; the economic, social, and geographical background. These, I felt, constituted a whole, and this whole is the subject of this book.

The book covers the half-century since the end of World War I, and I have attempted to portray not only the remarkable changes that have occurred in the industry, but also the moods that accompanied those changes. The technical descriptions are intended to be such that any practically-minded person can broadly understand the machines and processes, and the developments that have occurred.

Although interested in all aspects, I am conscious of the bias of a technologist, and of one who has specialized in spinning and weaving at that. Doubtless this bias shows through. The lives of the people in the industry and the interaction of those lives with the changes that have taken place are an important part of the total picture, but to treat them really well would require more intimate and extensive contacts than I—and possibly any writing person—have had. Rather than pass over this subject I have made the best of such information as could be gleaned and of such experiences as I have had.

The information on which the book is based is derived partly from personal experience, partly from conversing with people and reading newspaper accounts of events, and partly from more solid documentary evidence. Information that is presented objectively would, I believe, be accepted as broadly correct by most people who know; opinions, and information that is more narrowly based on particular experiences, are signified by the use of the first person singular.

Statistical information has been taken from the Textile Council's *Quarterly Statistical Review*, the *Annual Abstracts*, and Dr. R. Robson's *The Cotton Industry in Britain* (Macmillan, London, 1957). The last is a comprehensive history of the industry up to about 1956, and is a mine of statistical and other information. Caroline Miles's *Lancashire Textiles: A Case Study of Industrial Change* (Cambridge, 1968) came too late to affect my book. It may be regarded as bringing Dr. Robson's book up to date.

Photographs for more than one-half of the plates, and some of the diagrams, were supplied by the Textile Council; some photographs and most of the diagrams were supplied by the Shirley Institute; and the photograph for Plate 39 was supplied by the Manchester Chamber of Commerce. I am grateful to these bodies and the officers concerned.

I have received help from many friends in the industry. They have supplied documentary material and, often without realizing it, information and ideas; they have commented on a draft of the book. For all this: much thanks! Most of all I thank many of my former colleagues at the Shirley Institute, for whom I hold feelings of affection as well as gratitude. With the support of Dr. D. W. Hill, the Director, I have enjoyed the benefit of many of the critical and other resources of the Shirley Institute for producing published matter, without having suffered the inhibitions that were inevitable when the Institute was implicated in responsibility for my writings.

I also express my admiration and appreciation for the constructive and understanding way in which the staff of the publishers have dealt with the book in the course of production.

October 1968   L. H. C. TIPPETT

CHAPTER 1

General View

The Lancashire textile industry of today has developed from the Lancashire cotton industry of before World War I by changes which, in retrospect, have added up to a revolution. In its heyday it was pre-eminent among the textile industries of the world and among the exporting industries of this country; now it is of modest size and, so far from being a predominating exporter, has a struggle to achieve even two-thirds of the home market (although its exports at about £M50 a year continue to make a useful contribution to the country's balance of payments). A large part of the industry was made up of independent firms of modest size, often family concerns; now it is dominated by a very few very large corporations. Formerly capital costs were low compared with labour costs; now the industry is regarded as being highly 'capital intensive'. It was called the cotton industry because of the fibre it used almost exclusively; now it uses man-made fibre extensively in addition to cotton and must be termed the Lancashire *textile* industry.

The Lancashire must be distinguished from the other textile industries of the country based on other natural fibres—wool, silk, flax, and jute. These also use man-made fibres but in ways which are strongly influenced by the processes appropriate to the natural fibres, and the industries remain distinct, technically as well as in their trade associations, trade unions, and location, although various developments are tending to blur the dividing lines. The Lancashire industry spins yarn and weaves and finishes cloth. The production of fabrics by so-called 'weft' knitting belongs to another, the hosiery, industry, and there is yet another small industry for producing ribbons, tapes, and other narrow fabrics.

Some people advocate a single textile industry for the country, covering all processes and fibres. As a step in this direction, the Cotton Board, a statutory body performing certain functions for the cotton industry, was replaced in 1967 by the Textile Council which covers 'producing man-made fibres and spinning, throwing, doubling, bulking or texturizing, weaving, warp knitting, finishing and converting of yarn or fabric containing not less than 85 per cent by weight of man-made fibres, cotton, silk or any mixture thereof'. Nevertheless, the Lancashire textile industry as described above continues to exist as a recognizable entity.

The industry is distributed over approximately the one-third of the county in the south-east corner, mostly in towns surrounding Manchester. It spills over the border into Cheshire, Derbyshire, and Yorkshire, but in this book these areas are regarded as part of the Lancashire textile area. There are also factories producing the textiles Lancashire produces in Southern Scotland, Northern Ireland, Cumberland, the Midlands, and Southern England. For some purposes (e.g. the administration of Acts of Parliament) these are included in the Lancashire textile industry, for others (e.g. the organization of labour into unions) they are separate. However, since most of the activity (probably about nine-tenths) takes place in Lancashire and the adjacent areas, and all areas have had much the same experience, it is not often necessary to distinguish between county and country when referring to the industry.

The Lancashire cotton industry was eminent among British industries from many points of view. Its early history and its place in the industrial, social, economic, and political development of the country during the nineteenth century have been described in many places, and many aspects of that history are a part of the history taught in schools.

During the early years of this century the industry expanded enormously, largely to make goods for export to all parts of the world, until by the outbreak of World War I it had reached a very proud position. It had about 40 per cent of the world's capacity for producing textiles—there were said to be as many spindles in the Oldham district as in France and Germany together, and half as many as in all the U.S.A.[1] Over 60 per cent of cotton goods that entered into world trade were made in Lancashire. It was among the largest of British industries as measured by the number of people employed. In 1912, over 600,000 were employed in spinning, doubling, and weaving, and to these must be added those employed in

---

[1] *Scientific Research in relation to Cotton and the Cotton Industry*, Provisional Committee on Research and Education for the Cotton Industry, Manchester, 1917, p. 6.

finishing (probably over 100,000) and in ancillary trades making textile accessories and providing services. About one-quarter of the value of exports from the U.K. was attributed to cotton yarn and cloth. Over 85 per cent of the industry's output was exported, and it was said that the industry could satisfy the home market by the work done before breakfast (in the one-shift day there was then a pre-breakfast spell) leaving the rest of the day to satisfy the foreigner.

The growth had been rapid and easy, and had produced in the industry a strong sense of security and complacency. These and the pride are disclosed in the following statement made in 1912:

> For more than a century the cotton industry of Lancashire has held a position that has practically been unassailable by its foreign competitors. By slow and tedious methods improvement after improvement and invention after invention have so developed the various processes of manufacture that now the organisation of the whole industry is in a highly perfected state.
>
> Not only have the manufacturing processes received the careful attention of the cleverest and highest skilled workers but the question of the distribution of the finished article has also received the consideration to which its importance entitles it. The network of organisations radiating from Lancashire penetrates to every part of the globe. There is no country nor island, however remote, that is not in constant communication with the shipping houses by whom the distribution of cotton goods is effected. Vast amounts of capital and great concentration of energy have been required to build up the system of providing and retaining the markets upon which Lancashire is so largely dependent.[1]

The only anxiety seemed to be over the supply of raw cotton.

BETWEEN THE WARS

At the end of World War I the world was hungry for textiles and there was a boom in trade. Much of Lancashire seemed to go mad. Prices soared and enormous profits were made. Mills were recapitalized at very enhanced values. The margin for spinning a medium yarn, i.e. the difference between the cost of the fibre and the price received for the yarn, which in 1912 had been 3*d.* a pound, rose to 30*d.* in early 1920, and in that year 150 companies paid an average dividend of 40 per cent. One spinning master was said to have counted it for virtue that he did not succumb to the madness of selling out his business, whereas in truth he refused as inadequate

[1] Ernest H. Taylor, 'The problem of the cotton supply', *Journal of the Textile Institute*, 3, 1912, p. 44.

offers of six times the original value, and in holding out for more, held out too long.[1]

His holding out was too long because in 1921 the bubble burst. The demand for textiles slumped and although there were ups as well as downs in subsequent years, it never recovered to its pre-war level. Output of cloth had been 8,000 million yards in 1912; in 1930 it was 3,500 million and by 1937, a relatively good year, had recovered to only a little over 4,000 million. Thus after the boom and slump, the industry between the two wars produced at best at about one-half the pre-war rate. The reduction was largely in exports, which in 1937 were below 30 per cent of the pre-war rate. Output for home consumption fluctuated considerably but on the whole did not decline. In 1937 it was at roughly twice the pre-war rate, and even exceeded exports.

At first the 1921 reduction in demand was regarded as temporary. According to one view, dear cotton made the goods too expensive for the poor people of the East and demand would revive when American cotton came down in price—one shilling a pound was the figure first mentioned, but when that was reached and trade did not revive 10d. became the magic figure. The view was abandoned when 8d. cotton failed to revive trade. Another view was that the world's millions would continue to need cotton goods in large quantities and that the foreigner could not make them to compete with Lancashire. Lancashire had a suitable climate and operatives with inherited skills, and these were thought by some people to be permanent, decisive advantages. This view was nonsense. Strong cotton textile industries had been growing, notably in India and Japan, over decades, and Lancashire's share of international trade was declining even while the absolute amount was growing. The signs of the post-war decline were there before the war, had anyone the acumen to see them and the persuasiveness to alert Lancashire to them. The textile machinists had been exporting spindles and looms, and given the equipment, the spinning and weaving of at least 'bread and butter' yarns and cloths are not difficult. Further, labour represented an important part of the cost of converting cotton into cloth at the time and Lancashire could not counter the effect on cost of abysmally low wages in Eastern countries by any increases in efficiency that were then conceivable.

India, including the part that later became Pakistan, had been a very large market for Lancashire cloths, especially dhotis, but was

[1] B. Bowker, *Lancashire under the Hammer*, Hogarth Press, London, 1928.

establishing a large cotton industry as part of its economic development. This was partly financed by British capital, it was equipped
with machinery made in Lancashire, and some of the mills were run
under managers and supervisors who had emigrated from Lancashire.
The decline of the market was accelerated when India was given
fiscal autonomy in 1921 and subsequently imposed tariffs. Many of
the mills in Blackburn were at the time devoted to the manufacture of
dhotis, and to go into these mills shortly after a marked increase in
these tariffs and see the resulting emptiness of the looms was to gain
an acute sense of contact with world affairs. In a few years this trade
largely disappeared. The impact of Japanese competition in world
markets was felt in cotton textiles as in other manufactures; the large
China market was largely lost. Japanese competition continued to be
the bogey of the inter-war years. Cotton industries of smaller, but
significant for Lancashire, size grew also in other countries such as
those in South America.

At this time Gandhi visited Lancashire and was shown the heavy
concentration of mills and how the livelihood of the workers
depended on the mills' being kept working. A member of the party
that showed him round told me that Gandhi remained more concerned about the much greater poverty to be encountered in India. It
has been one of Lancashire's misfortunes that so much of its prosperity depended on the custom of the poverty-stricken masses of
underdeveloped countries. A more realistic, but no more effective,
approach was the attempt that was made during the 1930s to increase
the amount of Indian cotton consumed in Lancashire. The scope for
doing this was, however, small since the short staple of the cotton
made it suitable for only the coarser and lower quality yarns, and
only a small part of Lancashire's spinning machines had small
enough drafting rollers to cope with the short staples.

It took some time for the permanence, and perhaps the inevitability,
of the changes to be accepted in Lancashire. But at no time between
the wars was it remotely conceived how far the changes would go. At
first the firms acted independently to meet the supposedly temporary
situation. Many industrialists, even when they began to realize how
things were going, hung on for as long as they could, hoping that
other, weaker firms would go out of business first so that they would
survive to share in a more prosperous if smaller industry. We may
surmise that some directors of firms hung on more or less in order to
retain their means of livelihood. Unpaid fractions of shares were

called in—at one time owners of such shares would give money to people who would take such shares off their hands. Loans were raised from various sources including banks and working people. In the scramble for business prices were cut until they did little more than cover running costs, thus causing capital to run down and weakening the stronger firms that would survive. The weaker firms went out of business and some of the machinery was reconditioned and sold to foreign competitors of Lancashire. Such machinery had a value at a time of technical stagnation in the textile world.

One development that caused heartburning in parts of the industry, and continued to do so until the early years after World War II, was the debasement of cloths. In order to cheapen costs, well-established cloths would be gradually reduced in quality by slight and piecemeal reductions in the number of threads per inch and in the tex of the yarns, until the cloths became unsatisfactory, and the reputation of the industry suffered. Each step in this process was imperceptible, but the cumulative effect was bad. This was different from the defensible policy of designing a cheap cloth for a market where quality requirements were low.

The depression did not hit all parts of the industry or all areas of the county equally. The spinners of medium yarns in the Oldham area were badly affected, those of fine yarns, largely in the Bolton area, suffered but little. Weavers of fine cloths, many of them in the Nelson area, continued to be reasonably prosperous, being more affected by the ups and downs of home and Western trade than by the fall in exports to the East. Similar remarks may be made of the spinners and weavers of textiles for industrial uses, many of them in the Rochdale area. Condenser spinners and weavers, who process the waste cotton produced in ordinary manufacture, many of whom are in the Rossendale Valley, seem never to have suffered the depressions of the other sections of the industry, although they would be unlikely to admit that their history is one of uninterrupted prosperity.

The fortunes of individual firms depended a good deal on market connections. Some firms, when their markets declined, made other textile goods, but the possibilities in this direction were dependent on the ability of the managements, the acumen of the salesmen, and the technical situation, and were limited by the size of the market for all textiles. Some firms found salvation in the growing use of rayon.

The finishing section of the industry was less affected because foreign competitors did not develop the finishing processes as quickly or as competently as they did spinning and weaving. Much cloth woven abroad was finished in Lancashire and re-exported. Nevertheless the finishers had their difficulties, but the section was (and is) tightly organized and dealt with its difficulties quietly. The affairs of finishers have never received the public concern and debate accorded to those of spinners and weavers—at least not until they became the subject of an inquiry by the Monopolies and Restrictive Practices Commission in 1954 (see Appendix).

Gradually there arose in the industry a feeling that the *laissez-faire*, firm-by-firm approach to its problems was not enough. Remedies for 'Lancashire' were discussed in both the county and the country. In 1925 the Joint Committee of Cotton Trade Organizations was formed to help the discussions and crystallize them into action, and in 1927 this established the Cotton Trade Statistical Bureau to provide information. These have made a permanent mark on the services available to the industry. In 1930 there was a report of a Government Committee under the chairmanship of J. R. Clynes. Even at that time the emphasis in the report was on reviving the Lancashire trade, and restoration of something approaching its pre-war prosperity was implicitly regarded as a realistic objective. A public acceptance of the decline would presumably have been stigmatized as defeatist. The 1946 Cotton Working Party Report states:[1]

> Many attempts to reorganise the industry were made. Apart from direct Government assistance by subsidies and tariffs, all the methods used by other British industries in similar circumstances were tried in Lancashire. Price-fixing associations, regulation of output by quotas, amalgamations, redundancy schemes and special marketing methods were all considered and occasionally put into practice. Compared with similar measures in some other industries they met with more opposition within the trade and even when effectively applied were less successful in restoring a degree of profitability.

The strong, free-trade, *laissez-faire* tradition of the industry died very hard and provided a resistance to corporate action. Gradually there grew a feeling that statutory support was necessary to give effect to the wishes of the majority in the industry.

There had been some amalgamation of mills and works into large firms about the turn of the century, but the industry was mostly made up of small firms, and further amalgamation was thought to be a good thing—'rationalization' was the magic word. The urge for

[1] H.M.S.O., London.

B

amalgamations was strongest in the spinning section. In 1929 the largest spinning combine in the world, the Lancashire Cotton Corporation, was formed through the influence of the banks. At the outset this had about one-seventh of the spinning spindles of the industry. Other, smaller combines were formed, and some of these included a significant amount of weaving.

A reduction in machinery to match the reduction in demand was seen to be the first necessity for a restoration of profitability, but this had not occurred. By 1930, the acquisition of new spindles had exceeded losses, and looms had been reduced by only about one-tenth. The working of economic forces had entailed much human misery, which economists are not able to bring into the account, but it had not been effective in cutting down the size of the industry. Subsequently the larger combines scrapped machinery in accordance with one of the objectives of their formation. Between 1930 and 1939 the Lancashire Cotton Corporation reduced its spindles by nearly one-half. Under the Cotton Spinning Industry Act of 1936, a Spindles Board was formed to eliminate spindles and spread the cost over the industry by means of a levy. As a result of all actions, by 1937 spindles and looms were reduced by about one-third of their 1912 numbers; but output had been reduced by about one-half.

Operatives also were redundant, but their numbers declined by less than one-tenth up to 1930 and about one-third up to 1937. No co-operative attempts were made to deal with this other than by the national provision of the 'dole'. Consequently, unemployment rates were high. When, in 1924, the national percentage was 10, the cotton percentage was 16; the corresponding figures for 1930 were 17 and 45; for 1937 they were both about 10. There were not many alternative industries in the textile districts, and such as there were did not offer much opportunity for employment. The effects could be seen by walking through Lancashire towns and villages during these years, noting the dilapidated property, empty shops, and shops stocked with junk, and meeting people dressed drably. The effects on the personal life of the people can only be imagined. During the inter-war years the industry acquired a reputation as a bad one in which to work, a reputation which has contributed to post-war labour shortages.

To the misery of unemployment and short-time working was added that of strikes and lockouts. Employers attempted to meet declining trade and low prices by the time-honoured expedient of reducing wages, and in 1921, 1929, and 1932 there were stoppages (at this time it does not seem important to define whether they were strikes or lock-outs) of one to three weeks' duration in consequence. They were all settled by a reduction which was less than that originally proposed. In 1931 there was a four-week strike of weavers against the spreading 'more looms' system. The system, which was ultimately accepted and was the forerunner of the more radical post-war redeployment of labour, involved providing weavers with modest labour-saving facilities and increasing the number of looms per weaver from four to six or eight, with adjustments to wage rates resulting in an increased wage per weaver but a reduced wage cost per loom. In times of unemployment this was not popular with organized labour, and it was misused by some employers to disguise wage-cutting. Such misuse was ultimately prevented by a 1934 Act of Parliament which in effect legalized wage agreements in the weaving section of the industry. One result of the unrest of these years was the development of a procedure for settling disputes peacefully, and there has been no stoppage, other than an occasional one involving only one or two mills, since 1932.

There was not much technical development during the period. Single-process opening and high-draft spinning (these and other technical matters will be described in later chapters) and automatic winding were introduced, and automatic looms (a commonplace in the U.S.A.) were available, but these were adopted in only a few mills. They were mentioned in the various reports as technical improvements, the adoption of which would reduce costs (no evidence as to this was given) and help to arrest the decline in the industry. The firm of Tootal Broadhurst and Lee (as it was then) introduced its finishing process, for making cotton fabrics resist creasing in use, in the early 1930s; this was the starting-point for the many 'no-iron', 'easy care', and 'permanent press' finishes that have so improved the presentation of cotton clothing fabrics in the 1950s and 1960s. At about the same time two anti-shrink processes for cotton cloths became available.

During the period the first man-made fibres, viscose and acetate rayon, were increasingly used in the industry until by 1937 they comprised a little over one-tenth of the total fibre used. These fibres were produced for utilization by the textile industries based on natural fibres, although there are indications that this was regarded as a temporary measure, and that the rayon-producing interests expected a separate textile industry for processing rayon to develop

In the event this has not occurred. Of the traditional textile industries, the cotton industry has been by far the largest and most enterprising consumer of rayon.

The British Cotton Industry Research Association was founded at the Shirley Institute in 1919 and this took the lead in the process, which ultimately was decisively important in enabling the industry to cope with the technical changes that were to occur, of transforming cotton processing from a craft to a technology.

These developments affected a few mills, mostly in part only, and gave some novelty to Lancashire's products. But they had only a little effect on the main mass of the industry and its products. Technical development requires capital investment and a sense of progressiveness among managements. Because of low profits and obsession with the problems of week-to-week survival these were lacking between the wars. Looking back after the technical revolution that has occurred during the 1950s and 1960s, the industry seems to have been almost technically stagnant between the wars, but the seeds of the revolution were then sown.

All the activities of the 1930s for dealing with the industry's problems co-operatively culminated in the Cotton Industry (Reorganisation) Act, 1939. This provided for the setting up of the Cotton Industry Board with powers to administer and enforce schemes for eliminating redundant machinery and for specifying minimum prices for the industry's products. The Board was to set up an Export Development Committee, and had powers 'to perform certain services for the benefit of the industry', which were the services later performed by the Cotton Board and the Textile Council (see Chapter 5). Provision was made to ensure that the actions of the Board were in accordance with the desires of substantial majorities in the industry, and the oversight of the Board of Trade safeguarded the public interest. The Board was to have powers to raise the necessary finance by levies, and there was mention of Government subsidies. Owing to the war the Act was never operated, but it epitomized the mind of the industry and Government at the time on what should be done, and foreshadowed many of the things that were done after the war.

WORLD WAR II

With the approach and outbreak of the war, commercial difficulties disappeared. Demand, especially for military stores such as uniform material, canvas, webbing, and balloon fabric, was high, and prices were more than adequate. Early in the war the Cotton Control was established to secure and regulate the supply of cotton and other raw materials, and to regulate production so as to meet the country's needs. Early in 1941 the Government decided that cotton could not be supplied to keep all Lancashire's mills running, that many of the operatives were required for making munitions, and that the country would have to make do with a restricted output. Some mills, chosen by Government officials, were closed, their buildings being used for the storage of food and other commodities, and production was 'concentrated' into so-called 'nucleus' mills. The machinery in the 'concentrated' mills, as the closed ones were called, was taken care of at the charge of the nucleus mills. About 38 per cent of the spinning spindles were taken out of production and the number of operatives was reduced by nearly one-half as compared with 1937.[1]

The industry was also very closely controlled, largely through the Cotton Control and the Cotton Board (the latter had been foreshadowed in the 1939 Reorganisation Act), which had been set up in 1940, in the quantities and types of its products. The requirements of the services were specified by systems that had been developed over many years. For civilian consumers the Cotton Board developed a so-called 'utility scheme' according to which a range of cloths was specified that were considered to meet consumers' needs efficiently and economically. The scheme facilitated control and price regulation, promoted efficient manufacture by providing long runs of standard lines of goods, and provided the consumer with good value for money.

Technically the period was one of adaptation to changed circumstances. Unfamiliar growths of cotton had to be used as the sources of supply varied. For example, early in the war American cotton had to be used sparingly because it cost dollars, and the emphasis was on using Egyptian and Indian cottons where possible. Later, long staple Egyptian cotton became scarce and for some purposes spinners had to use East African and American cottons instead. Sago starch had been the sizing adhesive most commonly used by weavers; it became scarce at times and maize (corn), farina (potato), or tapioca (manioc) had to be substituted. Flax became scarce and ways had to be found of making cotton serve instead where hitherto flax had shown special

[1] R. W. Lacey, 'Cotton's War Effort', *Transactions of the Manchester Statistical Society*, November, 1946.

advantages (in making fabrics required to be impervious to water). Silk had to be substituted by the new fibre, nylon, in parachute fabrics, and Lancashire manufacturers shared in doing this. This experience proved to be of permanent advantage.

POST-WAR RECONSTRUCTION

When the war ended the closed mills were 'de-concentrated', presumably more an act of justice than a result of calculations showing that the country would need all the equipment. Normal commercial ways of determining what yarns and fabrics should be produced were gradually restored. The utility scheme was thought by some to hamper commercial enterprise in developing fabrics for the market but it survived until 1952. However, there was no attempt to return fully to the free-market conditions of the 1920s. Inter-war experiences were not forgotten, and planning and control were in accord with the spirit of the times.

The public control of the supply of raw cotton was the policy of the new Labour Government, and the Cotton Control became the Raw Cotton Commission in 1947. It was the sole agency in the country for importing and distributing raw cotton until 1954, when it was liquidated and the Liverpool and Manchester markets were re-opened.

For a few years the world demand for Lancashire's products outran the industry's ability to supply. Prices were good, profits were easily made, and production was the problem. However, the wild financial operations of 1920 were not repeated. Some firms invested in new equipment, some in securities or in other industries.

The limiting factor to production was the labour supply. Many operatives who had been removed from the industry during the war did not return, and the reduced labour force was ageing. An intensive recruiting campaign by the Cotton Board had to counter the unfavourable view of the industry caused by the inter-war experiences, and 'displaced persons' from Central Europe were recruited. Many of these have happily settled in the county. Attempts were made to generate some enthusiasm for the industry by such means as exhibiting posters with the legend: 'Britain's bread hangs by Lancashire's thread'. These efforts only brought the numbers in 1953 to about 70 per cent of the 1937 numbers.

The influx of new operatives and the need to make them effective quickly showed the need for improved training methods. The traditional method had been to put the newcomer, usually a juvenile, to work alongside an experienced operative, whose knowledge and skill, plus bad practices, were slowly communicated. To meet the new situation systematic methods of training, involving a breakdown of the jobs and instruction and practice in the parts, were developed, and many mills established small training sections or 'schools' separated from the main production. This has become a permanent feature of the industry.

Labour shortage gave impetus to the movement, which was started during the war, for making mills pleasanter places to work in. Hitherto, little regard seems to have been paid to the people who had to work in the mills. Many mills were dingy inside, walls were lime-washed to a dismal bluish shade, floors of weaving sheds were often uneven and slimy from the dampness of the conditions, as much machinery as possible was crowded in (I have had to edge sideways along an alley between looms and even so have been touched in the stomach and back by the picking sticks that oscillate to and fro), there was much noise and dust, and artificial lighting was very poor. The usual facility provided for operatives to take food on the premises (a necessity when breakfast had to be taken at the mill) was a steam kettle for providing hot water in a lobby or other convenient place with a near-by barrel into which spent tea-leaves could be emptied (very smelly it became before receiving its periodical cleaning). The regulations under the Factory Acts did little more than prevent conditions from becoming lethal. Conditions were better than this at some of the newer mills, and some employers were more beneficent than others, but the conditions described were very common up to 1939.

After the war improvement was rapid. Mills were redecorated. Committees of employers, trade unionists, and factory inspectors laid down reasonable standards of spacing of machinery, lighting, ventilation, and other conditions. Canteens became almost universal, and some mills had nurseries where the infants of mothers working in the mill were looked after. Proper first-aid and medical services and rest-rooms were provided. Welfare officers were employed, and in many mills social events were organized. In short, the industry was largely brought up to date in these matters. Unfortunately, noise and dust presented more intractable problems, although these conditions were mitigated by the improved spacing and ventilation.

Another line of attack on the problem created by labour shortage was to increase labour productivity, for which there seemed to be (and there still is) considerable scope in the Lancashire textile as in other industries. At a Cotton Board conference in 1947 the possible increase was cautiously estimated at 10 to 20 per cent for the immediate future and 'in still more substantial proportions' for the longer term.

One way of achieving this was by re-arranging the allocation of operatives to machines—'redeployment' was the term used. Stereotyped systems for manning the spindles and looms had grown up over decades, and these, if ever they were really efficient, had in many places been rendered inefficient by even such modest technical developments as had taken place. Redeployment was hailed as one way of increasing productivity. The movement for this had started in the 1930s when in some mills the weaver's complement of non-automatic looms had been increased from the traditional four to six or eight. This movement was quickened, and extended to spinning and winding, and was more professionally operated than before with the aid of work study. Increases in productivity were also helped by improvements in the lay-out of mills, by the provision of modern equipment for handling and transporting material in process, and so on.

The campaign for encouraging these developments was vigorous —it had almost the fervour of a religious revival. Lectures advocating them and expounding their principles were given up and down the county; industrialists who had successfully redeployed gave papers at conferences describing their experiences; the main trade associations for spinning and weaving appointed technical officers specially to help their members in these fields; an experiment was done at Musgrave Mill, Bolton, to demonstrate the advantages of redeployment; courses of instruction in work study were set up; mills employed consultants to develop particular schemes. The need for securing the co-operation of the operatives was fully recognized, and the new doctrines were addressed as much to trade unions as to managers. The early response varied according to the union and district, ranging from implacable opposition, through acquiescence, to active co-operation. Some union officers conscientiously objected to the work study that was involved, holding that the associated timing of the operatives was an affront to human dignity. Others even pushed managers along the road. Mills made their own arrangements for securing the co-operation of their operatives; some established joint consultation committees, but these do not seem to have had much vogue. In all this activity, the Cotton Board played a prominent part.

The systems by which the wages of the operatives were calculated, which had developed over many decades and had become very elaborate and rigid, were thought to be unsatisfactory. They resulted in some operatives being comparatively well paid for doing less work than others who were comparatively ill paid, and took inadequate account of the production facilities provided, and so tended to discourage the provision by management of labour-saving equipment. They also failed to provide the operatives with incentives to accept redeployment. The Government appointed commissions to examine these matters, and as a result new wage systems were adopted for spinners and weavers.

Labour productivity was also increased by developments in the basic textile machinery. At first it was thought that these would be effective only in the long run, since new machines would take a long time to procure, especially in the early post-war years. Redeployment, on the other hand, could be immediately effective. In the event appreciable increases in productivity in the industry as a whole only began to appear in the late 1950s after a considerable amount of re-equipment as well as redeployment had taken effect. Redeployment and the adoption of new management practices involve changing the mental attitudes of and giving training to many people. These take time, and often can only take place when a new situation is created by the installation of new machinery.

All this activity occurred against a background of belief, held by the Government and the public at large, that the industry was inefficient and needed radical modernization, and that its revival was of national importance. When the war broke out, the industry was a 'problem child'; it remained so. Even people in the industry accepted that improvements were possible and necessary. Consequently there were a number of official and semi-official commissions of inquiry. The commissions on wage systems (there were three) and the committees on conditions in the mills have been mentioned. In 1944 the Platt Mission made recommendations as a result of a visit to the U.S.A. to see how things were done there, and in 1949 teams made similar visits under the aegis of the (then) Anglo-American Council on Productivity. In 1945 a Cotton Working Party was appointed to survey all the problems of the industry and make recommendations, and its Report is a most comprehensive statement. It also discloses the controversial nature of the subject—there are nearly thirty pages of dissent from and qualifications of the main recommendations, written by members of the Working Party. All these bodies consisted of representatives of employers, labour, and the outside world. The United Textile Factory Workers' Association also made their own inquiries in 1943 and 1957, and issued reports. Has any industry ever been so investigated?

Until 1951 the industry was engaged in the congenial task of reconstructing itself as a production unit. All the goods that could be made could be sold. (There was much redundant machinery but that only gave trouble later.) Production problems can be faced without depression of the spirit, and if any people had misgivings about the future they did not destroy the prevailing sense of optimism.

After 1951 recession set in. Output of cloth had risen to 3,000 million lineal yards by 1951; in 1952 it fell to 2,300. Thereafter output fluctuated about a falling trend and in 1967 was about 1,300 million yards. Except that there was no massive long-term unemployment, there was a return of the depressing problems of the inter-war years resulting from falling markets and excess productive capacity. Exports, which had been about one-half of output in 1937, did not offer a solution. They fell to about one-third of the smaller output in 1951, and in 1967 were about one-sixth of the output of that year.

The situation was met in three ways. First, attempts were made to maintain prices and prevent the 'weak selling' of the inter-war years. Yarn prices had been statutorily controlled during the war and early post-war years, and when this ceased, in 1949, the Yarn Spinners' Association, which was a voluntary body containing virtually all spinners, established its own system. This was adhered to successfully —almost passionately by some spinners—until 1959, when the Restrictive Trade Practices Court ruled that it was contrary to the public interest. Attempts to establish corresponding schemes for weavers were less successful. Rayon weavers worked one for some years, but the larger body of cotton weavers failed to establish one in spite of trying hard. How far the failure was due to the technical difficulties of establishing standard prices for the wide and complex variety of

cloths produced, and how far to the difficulty of organizing disciplined action in a body containing many small firms, is a matter for
conjecture. The finishers had had a long and complicated history of
co-operative action for regulating production and maintaining
prices, and were able to protect themselves during the years following
1951. Among the finishers, calico printers operated a quota scheme
for distributing the business that was available until in 1954 the
Monopolies Commission condemned it.

The second way of meeting the decline in trade was by eliminating
redundant machinery. Over the years, many pressures had been
added to ordinary economic pressures, certainly from 1930 onwards.
One objective of the amalgamation of firms was to concentrate
production in efficient mills and works and eliminate redundant ones:
the Lancashire Cotton Corporation and the Calico Printers' Association are notable examples; and the Government subsidy for re-
equipment in spinning mills under an Act passed in 1948 was only
given to combinations of mills in the expectation that production
would be concentrated in some of the units of each combine. Several
schemes were from time to time evolved for providing funds to buy
up redundant machinery, but these did not come to much. In spite of
these pressures, the decline in the machinery in the industry did not
overtake the decline in trade, and in the 1950s seldom was more than
70 per cent of the machinery in place used. The position would be
aggravated by the extension of multi-shift working that was taking
place. In 1959 Parliament passed an Act providing for the collection
from the industry of a levy, the proceeds of which were used to buy
redundant machinery for destruction, and the Government gave a
subsidy to aid well-conceived schemes of re-equipment. The scale of
operation was large, and the effects were dramatic. Famous firms,
old-established and apparently well founded, went out of business.
One was Fielden Bros. of Todmorden, an early member of which was
the 'great master cotton spinner' of the history books and at one
time M.P. for Oldham, who was prominent in the agitation of the
early nineteenth century for the Ten Hours Bill. Another was the
firm of Horrockses, Crewdson & Co. Ltd., which has been absorbed
by a merchanting firm and whose enormous mills near the centre of
Preston are now closed—I have seen cloths bearing the name
Horrockses that were not made in the United Kingdom. In 1959
there were 15 million spindles and 220,000 looms in place; by 1961
the numbers had fallen to 9 million spindles and 150,000 looms. The

percentage of installed machinery in use rose from about 70 in 1959 to 90 in 1961. The scheme had quickly and substantially reduced the physical size of the industry without disrupting production. Any difficulties in securing supplies of the less common types of cloth were soon overcome.

The third, and not very effective, way of attacking the decline in trade was by agitating against the growing imports of cloth. While the markets could take all that Lancashire could produce, little public attention was paid to imports, but when the decline set in people noticed how large they were and how rapidly they were growing. For 1950–53 they averaged 300 million square yards or about one-ninth of the home output; they rose to 870 million in 1961, or about one-half of home output. Most of this cloth came from Hong Kong, India, and (later) Pakistan. Wages were very low in those countries, and since they were in the Commonwealth there were, in accordance with the Ottawa Agreement of 1932, no tariffs to protect against these competitors. The industry became alarmed as it saw itself being displaced so considerably even on the home market and agitated for Government intervention. But the Government was reluctant to act. Doubtless there were difficulties over introducing tariffs, and the Government also wished to help the developing countries by accepting their manufactured products. Possibly also it regarded the industry as being too large through carrying inefficient units. But people in the industry had (and still have) a sense of grievance. Granted that developing countries needed help—why should all the burden fall on the Lancashire textile industry? The industrialist's cup of indignation overflowed when, having decided that some piece of new foreign machinery met his needs more efficiently than the British counterpart did, he found that he had to pay an import duty on it. Had the Government written the industry off? No politician dared to say that this was so, but subsequent events were consistent with the view that the Government had written off a large part of it. The industry publicized its case, and deputations visited London and the exporting countries. But the only results were the 1959 Act and help in arriving at agreements with the three countries limiting imports from them into the United Kingdom. At the time of writing (1968) such limits apply, although they are uncomfortably high and do not stop the effects of very low prices. Portugal has become another source of cheap imports that are troubling the industry.

The decline of the industry since World War II has not been accompanied by as much social distress as that following World War I. Other industries have expanded or moved into the districts and have provided jobs, and except for short periods and in a few areas the prevailing feature of the industry has been (and is) a shortage of operatives. The application of the 1959 Redundancy Act provided compensation for displaced operatives, and this must have eased things, although there is evidence[1] that the provision was not much used. Since 1952 the unemployment percentage in spinning and weaving at the mid-year count has fluctuated between 0·6 and 8·0, with an average for fourteen years of 2·8. Of course there have been the discomfort and even hardship of changing jobs. Mule spinners, in particular, are highly skilled workers and have no market for their skills when unemployed. Some take more lowly jobs in the mill and mitigate the loss in wages by working on night shifts. Managers too have shared the distresses of redundancy.

Other industries have used some of the vacated mills. Between 1951 and 1963, 600 mill buildings became vacant of which about two-thirds were already re-occupied by 1963.[2]

The general cut-back in industrial activity of 1966 hit the industry very hard, and there is no assurance that the industry will not decline further despite the relief given by a welcome revival of trade in 1968. The position reached in 1967, compared with that of 1912 and 1937, is shown by the very approximate figures in the table on p. 20. Most of the traditional industry has gone, but there remains a substantial industry. How far it can be regarded as a new one will be examined in the next section.

A NEW INDUSTRY?

While the politicians and commercial people in the industry were meeting the frustrations and discouragements of the 1950s and 1960s, directors responsible for investment, technologists, managers, trade association officials, and trade unionists were working to bring the industry up to date and make it more efficient.

---

[1] Joseph King of the National Association of Card, Blowing and Ringroom Operatives, writing in the *Guardian*, 24 March 1964.
[2] E. G. Allen, 'Post-war development in Lancashire and Merseyside', *Trans. Manch. Statist. Soc.*, November 1963.

	1912	1937	1967
Operatives employed in spinning, doubling, and weaving, *thousands*	620	360	100
Spinning spindles in place, *million ring equivalent*	40	26	4½
Looms in place, *thousands*	790	520	92
Output of cloth, *million yards*	8,000	4,000	1,300
Cloth exports as percentage of output	86	47	14
Cloth imports as percentage of output	1	1½	66
Cloth exports from U.K. as percentage of world exports	66	28	3*
Exports of industry as percentage of value of all exports from U.K.	25	14	2†

* 1966.

† The value exported in 1967 of yarn and thread of cotton and man-made fibre staple, and of cloth of cotton and man-made fibre both staple and filament was £M53·5. In order to assess the contribution of the Lancashire textile industry to exports, this figure should be increased by the value of the yarn and cloth in made-up exports such as garments, and the whole reduced by the value in the exports of the imported cotton fibre and the man-made fibre and yarn which are supplied by another industry.

One direction was by vigorously adopting the new man-made fibres that were being produced, learning how to process them, and exploiting their properties to design and produce new fabrics. The pre-war cellulosic fibres, viscose rayon and acetate, are produced in several forms, and there are available also (in the terms of the chemist) polyamide fibres (nylons), polyester fibres ('Terylene' and 'Dacron' are two brands), acrylic fibres, and others. Each fibre has its own properties and potentialities, each its processing peculiarities. The producers have promoted their fibres vigorously and have given technical aid to processers, but they would have had little success without the backing of the textile processing industries. It is significant that two large producers, Courtaulds and I.C.I., have deemed it advisable to take a large financial interest in the Lancashire industry.

Of the filament yarn of man-made fibre produced in 1967 in the United Kingdom and not exported, 42 per cent was consumed in the industry, and of the staple fibre 30 per cent in 'cotton spinning'. Of the cloth produced by the industry in 1967, 42 per cent was of man-made fibres or mixtures containing man-made fibres, the remaining 58 per cent being of cotton alone. Some dedicated enthusiasts look forward to the day when man-made fibres will oust cotton entirely, holding that the cotton fields should be used to grow food. Mr. G. A.

Samuel of Courtaulds[1] does not go as far as this. He expects that the proportion of man-made fibres will increase, but that natural fibres will continue to have a substantial market. The Lancashire textile industry is ready to process all the fibres of whatever origin the market can be induced to demand.

Post-war developments in the finishing of cloth have been very great. Fabrics of new fibres have presented special finishing problems, especially of dyeing, which have been attacked. The current 'easy care' or 'no iron' finishes have transformed the presentation of cotton fabrics to the consumer.

Developments in textile technology over many years, and the quickening of the rate of application since the war, have much improved the reliability with which fabrics can be specified and produced to have the qualities required by the consumer; and quality control is an important function in the modern Lancashire mill or works. Improved technical contacts between spinners, weavers, and finishers, and even with garment makers in some instances, have also been important in this connection. For the domestic consumer this has been powerfully influenced by the multiple shops. These give very large orders which are much appreciated even at the keen prices offered, and the resulting commercial power coupled with technical competence enables them to exert a strong influence for quality control as well as efficient production. The firm of Marks and Spencer Ltd. have been pioneers in this movement, and this was recognized when the director of the firm most immediately responsible, Dr. Eric Kann, retired. At the instigation of several industrialists a presentation fund was established, and was well supported by people and firms in the textile industries, in recognition of Dr. Kann's services. At his request the money was used to establish in 1963 a scholarship, which bears his name and is administered by the Textile Institute.

The ability to produce cloths of high quality compared with competitors' products does not guarantee survival for a firm, but in a Western, high-wage textile industry survival is impossible without it. Enough of the Lancashire industry survives, and even flourishes, to show that in this respect the industry maintains a high position. Some of the technical developments referred to have originated abroad, and all are available to textile processers everywhere, but Lancashire is fully familiar with them and applies them vigorously.

[1] In 'Man-made Fibres', a *Guardian* Survey, March 1966.

Ever since the end of the war there has been a strong emphasis on re-equipment, and this has involved much more than replacing old ironmongery by new. Textile machinery has been continuously and radically improved in ways that will be described in a later chapter. New automatic mechanisms have been invented, including control systems for 'automation'; some machines have been speeded up, four- or fivefold or even more; the newer machines are mostly more labour-saving, and they are more reliable in producing yarns and cloths of high quality. The new machines have to be made with high engineering precision and so are much increased in cost beyond the increases occasioned by inflation. I am not aware of any meaningful information on the extent to which the industry has modernized its equipment (information on the money invested, for example, conveys little standing on its own). One indication is a report that the Courtaulds plan for re-equipping its spinning mills totals £12 million—one-third of the bid to acquire them. I have the impression that most mills have some new equipment (unless they are due to be closed) and some have much. Much old machinery remains, and lack of confidence in the future must have had a restraining influence on re-equipment.

Two machinery changes that are special to Lancashire are the replacement of mule by ring spinning, and of non-automatic by automatic looms. Mule spinning is the older, and now obsolete, form, and Lancashire was unique among the major cotton industries of the world in being largely based on it. No new mules have been installed since the early 1920s, and few since World War I, and the substitution by ring frames is now well advanced. As recently as 1959 there were almost as many mule as ring spindles in place; in 1967 under 15 per cent of the spinning capacity was in the form of mule spindles. In its former devotion to the non-automatic loom (it is termed the 'Lancashire loom'), the Lancashire industry was unusual but not unique, and replacement has not gone as far as in spinning. In 1959 about 80 per cent of looms were non-automatic; by 1967 this percentage had fallen to a little under 60. The changes in percentage are due more to the elimination of the older equipment than to an increase in the amount of the newer types.

Much has been done to modernize the management of the mills and works. The application of work study to labour deployment, and to increasing labour productivity generally, which began in the early post-war years, has continued with the agreement of the unions.

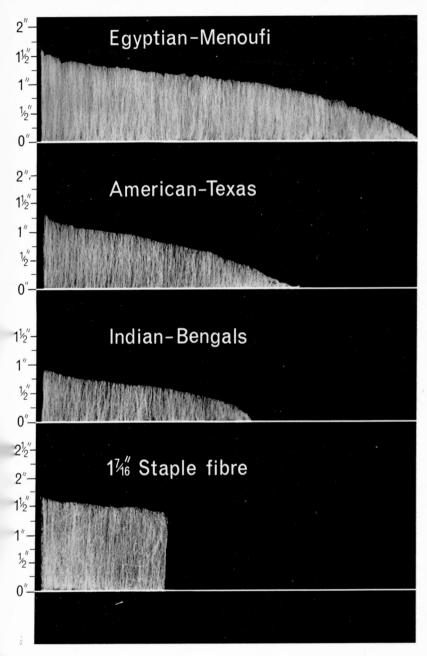

Plate 1. Arrays of fibres showing their lengths. The fibres in a small sample have been laid side by side, in order of length, on a plush pad. Those in the cotton samples vary from a little longer than the staple length down to quite short lengths. The staple fibre has been cut from rayon into fibres of substantially one length.

Many people at various levels in the management hierarchy have been trained in the techniques; there is less reliance than before on outside consultants to make once-for-all redeployments, and more routine use of work study to secure a continuing progress towards efficiency. This is important for the efficient use of new machinery. The attention paid to new management techniques has broadened to include the whole range available. Modern systems of cost, stock, production, and quality control; inter-firm comparisons; linear programming; productivity measurement: these are all known to most managers and are to be met in many mills. Management in the industry has always been well trained in technical matters; it is now better trained than it was in the arts of management, and is better equipped generally to bring about and cope with change.

The new wage systems for spinning and weaving that were introduced in the early post-war years were more effective than the old in justly rewarding effort and encouraging efficiency, and are still in use. But they do not meet the new situations created by modern technical conditions and are being superseded by agreements with the unions allowing for more flexible arrangements based on work study.

Lancashire has been notorious for the persistence with which it has adhered to single-shift working. Multi-shift working is now acceptable to the unions where new machinery is installed and physical conditions for the operatives are satisfactory, and two- and three-shift working is increasing. In 1967 about 46 per cent of spindles ran single shifts, 37 per cent ran two shifts, and 16 per cent ran three shifts. On average spindles and looms ran for about 60 hours a week. If the adoption of multi-shift working is progress, Lancashire has gone some way, but it has a long way to go before it achieves the 168 hours a week of 'round the clock' working or the 80–90 hours a week of some competing countries in Europe. In 1966 the average number of hours a year spinning machinery was run in each of a number of European countries was from 24 to 70 per cent greater than the average for Lancashire.

One fashionable measure of industrial efficiency is labour productivity, and since the Textile Council publishes figures of yarn and

---

Plate 2. Unloading bales of cotton at a mill. Part, at least, of the ragged appearance results from the extraction of samples.
Plate 3. Examining and classing cotton in the Cotton Exchange building at Liverpool. The people on the right are hand stapling.

cloth production and of people employed, some indications of the effects of all the changes of recent years are available. One difficulty is that the mixture of products changes so that it is hard to interpret comparisons over the years. This difficulty is, I believe, insurmountable for cloth productivity. Another difficulty is that no industry adjusts itself completely to short-term fluctuations; and good trade in one year tends to result in comparatively high labour productivity, bad trade in low. With these reservations in mind, I have examined the figures for spinning and think that the following results present a fair picture. Compared with the average for 1950-9 (for which years there was no discernible trend) the production of yarn in 1964-7 per operative at work per annum increased by 35 per cent if the weight of yarn produced is the measure, or 10 per cent if length is the measure (between the two periods the yarn became coarser on average). These figures are affected, perhaps to the extent of one-tenth, by a reduction in the hours worked each week. When it is remembered that in 1950 labour productivity in spinning mills in the U.S.A. was reported to have been twice that in the best 25 per cent of Lancashire mills, and that in 1965 the average productivity for each of a number of European countries was 27 to 70 per cent greater than the average for Lancashire,[1] the improvement in Lancashire seems to have been a meagre return for the effort expended.

The global figures cover a large variation from mill to mill, and there are bright spots. For example, Mr. G. H. Jolly reported in the *Guardian* of 24 March 1964 that between 1959 and 1963 labour productivity in the spinning mills of Combined English Mills (C.E.M.) increased by about 25 per cent, or 6 per cent per annum. It was later reported that during the same period the spindles ('ring equivalent') were reduced from 1·4 to 0·4 million in number. Production per 100 spindle hours increased by 40 per cent and this, together with additional shift working, enabled the total production of yarn to be maintained. After C.E.M. became part of Viyella International in 1964, it was possible to speed up the process of internal reorganization, and further improvements resulted. In the house magazine *Viyella International* (Autumn 1966) Mr. E. Cummins reports that in the subsequent three years production per employee per annum increased by 50 per cent and the average run-

---

[1] The references for these two statements are: *Report on Cotton Spinning*, British Productivity Council, London, 1950; and J. Lustig, 'Productivity in the spinning industry', *Textile Weekly*, 17 February 1967, p. 233.

ning hours per spindle per week increased from 59 to 100. Doubtless a fuller picture for the industry as a whole will emerge from the Textile Council's productivity study, started in 1967 (p. 117).

It seems that the Lancashire textile industry has been somewhat isolated and that the chief post-war contacts with other industries have been when textile firms have sought to diversify their activities by investing in non-textile activities, which, for a few firms, have become a predominating interest. But if the industry is to be re-equipped adequately, much new capital is required, and there can be no confidence in the future unless new and powerful financial resources can be made available. This was illustrated in a dramatic way through the mergers and 'take-overs' that took place round about 1964.

The pace was set by Viyella International Ltd., which had developed from an old-established textile concern and had large sums of money made available by I.C.I. During 1964 it acquired something like ten substantial companies, including Bradford Dyers' Association (£6·4 million bid) and Combined English Mills, a combine of spinners of fine yarns. English Sewing Cotton Company, also an old-established textile firm helped by money provided by I.C.I., and Courtaulds, the producer of man-made fibres and chemicals, and other smaller but substantial concerns were also absorbing companies. A notable merger was that of Tootal Broadhurst and Lee with English Sewing Cotton Company. Every few weeks in 1964 there was the announcement of another bid or merger. The dramatic climax came when, one morning in July, we read that Courtaulds had made a bid (which was successful) of £36 million for Lancashire Cotton Corporation and Fine Spinners and Doublers, which together controlled about one-third of the spinning spindles of the industry. In one year the industry was turned from one in which many small and medium-sized firms operated independently to one which is dominated by a few very large corporations. Independent firms continue to operate—more than twenty-five public companies are quoted on the stock exchanges and there are also private companies—but the structure of the industry has changed. Since 1964 there have been further mergers and changes in company structure, a notable one being the 1968 merger between English Sewing Cotton Company and Calico Printers' Association to form English Calico Ltd.

A feature of the recent mergers that is significant for the future is that each combine covers a wide range of textile processes from spinning to finishing, and reaches beyond the traditional Lancashire processes to knitting, garment making, and merchanting. Each combine is not necessarily balanced in all these functions—for example it would take a long time for Courtaulds to balance by its other processes the enormous spinning capacity it controls or Viyella to balance its finishing capacity—and much scope remains for interfirm commerce. Moreover it would be impracticable for each combine to be run as a single technical unit; there must be division into departments, and this tends to follow somewhat the lines of the processes, so that in the management much of the original 'horizontal' structure remains. But the combination into large comprehensive firms facilitates integration between processes, formal or informal, and softens the lines of the horizontal divisions, thus leading to the technical advantages of 'vertical' integration. It is apparent that this is happening. For example, in 1967 Courtaulds announced projects for building two new mills for weaving spun yarns, outside the main textile area, thus going some way towards balancing its spinning capacity.

Another significant feature of the mergers is the part played by the two large producers of man-made fibres, Courtaulds and I.C.I. This massive demonstration by outside industrial corporations of confidence in the future of the industry put heart into those already working in it.

CHAPTER 2
Products and Raw Materials

Some of the yarn produced in Lancashire is supplied to other textile industries: the hosiery industry, which takes about one-fifth of the output, the carpet industry, and the garment industry, which uses sewing thread. About 4 per cent is exported. Most is used in the Lancashire industry to produce woven cloth, most of which is in forms familiar to ordinary consumers: fabrics for clothing (including overalls and other protective clothing); fabrics for household use (sheetings, towellings, table-cloths, etc.); furnishing fabrics; and surgical fabrics. However, there is also a large output of cloth for industrial use: tyre fabric; canvas for wagon covers and tents; belting; filter fabrics; leather cloth; book cloth; shoe linings; tracing cloth; and so on.

It is the job of the cloth designer, as opposed to the artist who designs a print, to specify a cloth having the qualities required by the consumer. It may be required to have aesthetic qualities: to be smooth or rough in texture, soft and clinging or stiff; to be lustrous or matt in appearance; to be plain or patterned with, say, stripes or checks. In addition there will be functional requirements to be met in various degrees according to the intended use: weight; strength and durability; bulkiness; resistance to tearing, creasing, deterioration on exposure to sun and rain, soiling; moisture absorbency; waterproofness; heat insulation; fireproofness; degree of resistance to wind. All these qualities are determined by the fibres and other materials used, the structure of the yarns and cloths, and the finishing treatment given to the cloth. Ideally, it should be possible to measure the qualities and then to specify the particulars necessary to realize them, and much research has been done towards this ideal.

Methods of measurement are being developed, and as satisfactory ones become ready they are made the subject of a British or International Standard. Some of the qualities are difficult to define and measure. Soiling, for example, is a complex phenomenon involving contamination by greasy dirt, say, at collars and sleeve-cuffs in contact with the body; by air-borne soot and dust, especially in cities; by water-borne dirt, especially in rain; by particles of dirt attracted and held by electrostatic forces; and by dirt rubbed from dirty surfaces. To be of value, any measure must be such that it can be made in a laboratory in a short time, and it is difficult to devise for such complex phenomena such a measure to give results that correspond with what happens in everyday usage with all its variety. However, progress is being made in measuring most qualities that matter. Broad differences, at least, can be measured; research is being pursued and the control of quality is being achieved with increasing success. The ordinary consumer should not be deceived, however, by test results, say, in some advertisement, purporting to demonstrate the excellence of some cloth, nor by a report showing that one cloth is slightly better than another in some aspect of performance. Such information may be cogent, but it is very unlikely to be so.

Research is necessary to discover how the various material and processing particulars determine the cloth qualities. Again, although much has been done and knowledge is always increasing, existing knowledge is far from complete and there is a large element of trial and error in the development of cloths. Fibre producers, cloth manufacturers, and merchant-converters invest much money in this activity. Promising cloths are tried on the market experimentally and some fail (for example, some readers will remember the brief appearance of 'Terylene' stockings—'Terylene nylons' as they were popularly named). With the uncertainty of deciding which cloth is best for a given purpose and with the variety of consumers' tastes, there is room for several competing cloths to perform the same function. A shirting, for example, may be of cotton, or a man-made fibre, or a blend; it may be woven or warp-knitted. The commercial success of a cloth owes much to salesmanship as well as to technical excellence, except perhaps in some industrial uses where the technical requirements are specific and exacting (although even here salesmanship doubtless plays some part). Nevertheless technical information provides a basis for the designer, in the ways shown in the following sections. These sections are not a comprehensive guide to fibres, yarns, cloths, and finishes; they are intended to be illustrative.

In addition to the engineering or physical aspects of cloth design, there is for cloths with woven or printed patterns the artistic aspect, to which Lancashire pays considerable attention, as the existence and activities of the Textile Council's Colour, Design and Style Centre show (p. 117). Firms employ expert designers who have art and a sufficiency of technology, and they buy the designs of free-lance artists. There are courses with their accompanying diplomas in art schools and technical colleges, and opportunities are given for designers to seek inspiration from foreign travel. British cloth designs are sometimes criticized as being uninteresting and unadventurous as compared with those from abroad, particularly from some country that happens to be in fashion at the moment. It may be that most of the home-produced cloth on display in shops and stores is for the mass of people, who are apparently conventional in their tastes, whereas the imports that excite the admiration of an élite tend to be smaller lots of selected designs. Foreign designs add to the variety and interest of cloths available to the consumer, and some of them specially appeal to some people, but Lancashire would not admit that they are generally superior.

FIBRES

Fibres occur in two forms, staple and continuous filament. Staple fibres are short: cotton is about one inch or so, wool and flax are several inches, say, three or more. Continuous filament fibres are virtually endless: silk occurs, and man-made fibres are produced, in this form. Most man-made fibres are also cut into staple for processing on the cotton, wool, or flax spinning system, or for blending with the natural fibres. Broadly, a staple yarn is relatively soft and bulky and has a matt appearance; a 'filament' yarn (unless it has been 'bulked', as will be described later) is smooth, lustrous, and almost wire-like. These characteristics carry through to the cloth.

The main substance of cotton is cellulose, which is the main substance of vegetation generally. It is among the strong, durable, and cheap natural fibres. An outstanding quality is its 'launderability'. Cotton cloths can be washed repeatedly, and even be boiled or steam-sterilized, with only a slow deterioration, and repeatedly 'come up fresh' after such treatment. Although not as moisture-absorbing as wool it is among the more absorbent fibres and so continues to be used for towels, handkerchiefs, and some underclothing. Natural disadvantages for some uses are its susceptibility to creasing and to attack by mildew and bacteria under damp conditions, and its high inflammability. These can to some extent be overcome by finishing treatments.

Cotton is grown in many parts of the world, and the crops grown in different places, even in different districts of a country, and (for any one place) in different years, have differences in characteristics that are important to the technologist. These arise from the breeds of cotton planted, the soil and methods of husbandry, the weather, and the effects of diseases and insect pests. It is an important art of the spinner to know what cottons are available and to select those that are suitable for his purposes. If in addition he can pick up bargain lots that are satisfactory, so much the better.

The first technical description of a cotton is its staple length, or shortly its 'staple'. The fibres in a sample vary in length from a small fraction of an inch to something over one inch, and the staple is a kind of average length that is not far from the most frequent or most typical length. There are three main types of cotton: the Egyptian types, grown mostly in Egypt and the Sudan and having staples of around one and a half inches; the American types, grown primarily in the U.S.A. but also in Africa, Eastern Europe, and South America and having staples of around one inch; and Indian types, grown in India and Pakistan and having staples of around three-quarters of an inch (Plate 1). In addition there is the small Sea Island crop with staples around one and three-quarter inches, and cottons intermediate between the main types—African countries, for example, produce some cottons of one and one-eighth to one and a quarter inches staple. Generally, the longer staples tend to have finer fibres and can be spun into finer yarns. Yarns of Sea Island cotton are exceptionally fine and 'silky'. Most of the world's production and consumption is of American types. Within each type there are sub-types, usually (but not always) named after the place where they were grown. For example, Sea Island may be St. Vincent or Barbados; an Egyptian-type cotton may be Menoufi or Ashmouni or Giza 30 or Sudan Sakel; an American-type cotton may be Texas or Californian or Brazilian or Nigerian or Turkish; an Indian-type cotton may be Bengals or Oomras or Broach.

After its staple a cotton is appraised by the non-fibrous waste it contains, which consists of dust, leaf, and other debris from the growing field and constitutes up to 10 per cent by weight of the bale. Colour too may be important. There is a Peruvian cotton that is specially white, which, when blended with viscose rayon staple, forms a yarn that is very acceptable in hosiery fabrics that are used in the natural state, without finishing.

More refined appraisals which are becoming necessary under modern conditions involve measurements of fibre fineness, strength, and maturity. Maturity is important because drought or insect attack may halt the development of the fibre on the plant before it is fully mature, and such fibre can create difficulties in processing and give an inferior yarn.

The cotton in a bale is appraised by examining a sample, the extraction of which gives a characteristic torn appearance to the bale (Plate 2). In commerce cotton has been, and still is, appraised by skilled men who feel it in bulk, notice how the fibres feel when a tuft is pulled apart, and generally give a subjective assessment including an estimate of the staple. The procedure is termed 'hand stapling'. Instruments have been devised to measure some of the qualities assessed in hand stapling and additional qualities such as strength. The resulting information is more comprehensive and reliable than that given by hand stapling; it can be stored and used in research. But the tests are too slow for the quick decisions that have to be made in commerce, and hand stapling is likely to be the main basis for a long time (Plate 3). Test results are much used in mills in a supplementary way and, with the development of quick automatic methods of test that is occurring, their use is likely to extend.

Cotton waste is fibre that is a by-product of ordinary spinning or is broken down from waste yarn produced in winding and weaving, and is processed in a special, the 'condenser', section of the industry. The fibre is short in staple and the yarns produced from it in the condenser process are weak, soft, and fluffy. They are used to make curtain materials, which do not suffer much wear and tear, and the cheaper flannelettes, sheetings, and towellings, where the consumer accepts some reduction in durability for the sake of cheapness.

The idea of dissolving cellulose in a chemical solution and extruding it through very fine holes into a bath where the cellulose is coagulated into a fibre, was developed in several forms during the second half of the nineteenth century, but it is only in the twentieth that corresponding industrial processes have been developed, and only between the two wars that any quantity of fibre first became available to the textile industry. Cellulosic man-made fibres were first produced in filament form and were thought of and used as cheap substitutes for silk. Hence it became known as 'artificial silk'. The shorter term 'art silk' was possibly the 'ad-man's' attempt to gloss over the weaknesses of the fibre and give it a meretricious appeal to the consumer. The producers quite soon decided that the fibre should be considered in its own right and not as a substitute, and coined the name 'rayon' for the most common type—viscose rayon. Producers of all artificial fibres now term their products 'man-made' fibres because of the unfortunate connotations the word 'artificial' has had for them.

Viscose rayon is mostly made from wood pulp, and in the form of staple fibre it is rather cheaper than cotton. It is weaker and less durable than cotton when dry and becomes very weak on being made wet. It stretches more than cotton before breaking. It does not recover well from creasing or stretching (rayon stockings bagged at the knees and were never successful), but can be given a crease-resist treatment. It is more moisture-absorbent than cotton. With all its limitations and advantages, viscose rayon is used in far greater quantities than any other man-made fibre, and more is used as staple fibre than as continuous filament. In its simplest form it is smooth and lustrous, but it can be modified to have a matt appearance. Several modified forms have been produced by altering the details of manufacture to increase the dry strength and durability (strong viscose rayon has almost ousted cotton in the manufacture of tyre fabrics), to reduce the weakening on wetting (so-called 'polynosic' fibre is very like cotton in this and other properties—but it would be heresy to term it 'artificial cotton'), or to give the fibre bulk by crimping it (such fibre is specially suitable for carpets).

Acetate, which comes next to viscose rayon in age and popularity, is mostly made from 'cotton linters' (short fuzzy fibres unsuitable for spinning even on the condenser system), and the process leaves the cellulose molecule chemically modified. It is less moisture-absorbent than cotton or viscose rayon, it recovers better from creasing, and it is electrically insulating (the crackle of electric sparks as acetate underclothing is removed when undressing will be familiar to most readers). It melts when heated sufficiently. Another fibre in this class, 'triacetate', has somewhat similar properties, and can be 'heat-set' (see opposite). When cotton and viscose rayon on the one hand and acetate on the other are dyed together in the same bath the resulting colours are different. This is used to produce 'cross-dyed' effects by having yarns of two fibres arranged in stripes or having one fibre in the warp and the other in the weft.

The cellulosic man-made fibres are termed 'regenerated' fibres because the basic cellulose molecule is already there in the raw material. Another group of fibres coming later in time are synthetic, in the chemist's language, because their substance is built up from more elementary molecules in the raw materials, which are complicated organic substances derived largely from coal and oil.

The three main 'synthetics' are polyamide fibres or nylons (of which two types are in use), polyester fibres, and acrylic fibres. These names are chemists' terms—the technologist and consumer regard them as labels for groups of fibres having particular properties. All appear under a number of brand names. As a group, synthetic fibres differ markedly from cotton and viscose rayon in the following ways. They are outstandingly strong and durable; they absorb little moisture and are little affected in any property by wetting; they recover well from creasing and stretching so that garments made from them require little or no ironing after washing; they are highly electrically insulating; they are resistant to attack by bacteria and mildew, and are not enjoyed as food by insects; they are resistant to attack by many chemicals; they can be 'heat-set'. 'Heat-setting' involves stretching or deforming the fibre when hot and allowing it to cool in that state; the stretched or deformed state then remains set in the fibre, and in the yarn or cloth containing the fibre. This property is useful for such things as putting permanent pleats into garments. The different synthetics have these properties in different degrees and the special characteristics of each are exploited by designers. For example, as compared with nylon, polyester fibre has a 'high modulus at low strains'; i.e., it is relatively inelastic to the small stretchings and deformations that occur in ordinary usage, so that the yarns and cloths are somewhat stiffer ('crisper') and more bulky than those made from the softer nylon.

There are several synthetic fibres in addition to those mentioned which are not used in great quantities in Lancashire, although where they are used they are of course important. Among these are the so-called 'elastomer' fibres which have rubber-like elasticity and are useful in making fabrics for corsets, swim-suits, and so on. A very new development is the production of yarns from fibre made by splitting flat tapes or films of polypropylene. So far, these are mostly used outside Lancashire for purposes normally associated with sisal and jute.

Man-made fibres in continuous filament are supplied to the Lancashire industry in the form of yarn ready for use. Fibre for staple yarns is also originally produced in filament form. It seems odd, on the face of things, to cut the continuous fibre into staple and then spin it into yarn, but there are three good reasons for doing this. (1) The processes of producing 'tow' (a thick rope of continuous filaments), cutting it into staple, and spinning the staple are cheaper than that of producing filament yarn. (2) The distinctive properties of staple yarns are desirable for some purposes. (3) Different staple fibres, man-made and natural, can be blended to produce yarns with a variety of desirable composite properties at competitive prices. The producer can cut man-made fibre into any required staple length—a few standard lengths are supplied—and the product has the advantage that the fibres of any one staple have almost all the same length (Plate 1).

A handbook issued by the British Man-made Fibres Federation early in 1968 lists over sixty brand names of fibres made in different countries, classified into eight types (cellulosic, polyamide, and so on).

The producer of man-made fibres has within his control not only their substance but also their thickness, shape of cross-section, and distribution of elastic properties within the cross-section. Coloured cellulosic fibres are produced by having the dye incorporated in the spinning mix, the resulting colours being exceptionally resistant to fading. Of course it is practicable and economical to produce at any one time only a limited number of fibres, but the number and variety available is bewildering to all but people intimately concerned.

The synthetic fibres are expensive—say, three times the price of cotton in equivalent staple, but the difference is likely to decrease in time, or even to disappear, as methods of manufacture improve and the enormous development costs become discharged.

YARNS

The most elementary and basic description of a yarn is its size or fineness, or weight per unit length. For staple yarns this has traditionally been measured in Lancashire by the 'count', which is the number of hanks, each of 840 yards, that weigh one pound. Other countries have different count systems (the metric system obviously provides one basis), although the past predominance of Lancashire textiles has given the 'English count' a wide currency for cotton and related yarns. Other industries, both in the United Kingdom and elsewhere, processing other fibres have other traditional counting systems. For filament yarn the textile industries generally have adopted the silk system of sizing by the 'denier' which is the weight in grammes of nine kilometres of the yarn. With the interpenetration of the textile industries, both nationally and internationally, it is inconvenient to have so many systems, so under the aegis of the International Standards Organisation a new quantity, the 'tex', is being adopted. The tex is the weight in grammes of one kilometre of the yarn. The change from the traditional system is difficult because people still think in terms of count, trade conventions have been built around it, and there is a system of derived quantities based on it. It may be that future generations will be at home with tex. However it is measured, specification of the size of the yarn is the very foundation of yarn and cloth design.

Next in importance comes the degree to which the yarn is twisted or, shortly, the 'twist', measured in Lancashire by the number of turns or spirals per inch (presumably the pains of adopting metric measures for this quantity will have to be endured some day). Twist is essential in a staple yarn to give it cohesion and strength. The twist inclines the fibres slightly to the general direction or axis of the yarn, so that when the yarn is tensioned the tension in the fibres causes them to press against each other (in mathematical language the linear tension in the fibres has a transverse component) and the resulting frictional forces prevent the fibres from slipping past each other. If the twist is insufficient the frictional forces are insufficient and the yarn is easily pulled apart. Readers can easily study the phenomenon in a yarn of knitting wool by twisting and untwisting it, stretching it gently at the same time, and noting how at a sufficient twist the fibres seem to lock and the yarn has strength. When a sufficiently twisted staple yarn breaks most of the fibres also break, and the strength of the yarn is closely dependent on that of the fibres. A filament yarn, which usually consists of many fibres lying side by side, does not depend on twist for its strength, but some twist is usually inserted for other reasons.

A staple yarn becomes stronger as the twist increases up to a certain value, but it also becomes more compact or 'harder'. For some uses both qualities are required, but for others (hosiery for example) softness is required and a lower twist is specified even though the yarn is weaker.

If a yarn, staple or filament, is twisted beyond a certain point, usually above that for maximum strength in a staple yarn, it tends to snarl. Sometimes such a yarn is set, perhaps (if it is a synthetic) by heating and cooling, so that the snarling tendency is made latent. It is then processed further, and when the setting medium is removed in finishing the snarling tendency reasserts itself and the product develops a bulky texture. This phenomenon is the basis of some of the modern processes for 'bulking' or 'texturizing' synthetic filament yarns.

In addition to fineness (henceforth referred to as tex) and twist, there are other qualities of ordinary staple yarns that are required in different degrees according to the usage, but they are not at present so widely the subject of precise measurement and specification. They include: freedom from slubs and specks of foreign matter; freedom from local and long-term irregularities in thickness; hairiness; and strength.

The 'bulking' or 'texturizing' of filament yarns, which is done to counter the smoothness and hardness of the yarns as produced, is achieved in several modern processes in which the fibres are made to crimp or crinkle. They may be imagined as being set into the form of irregularly coiled springs. Such yarns can also be made to have a controlled degree of elasticity or stretch, and are much used in garments that are required to fit the body closely and yet give to its movements—ski-pants are an example. The process of bulking is not much done in Lancashire (the industry uses bulked yarn), but has been energetically adopted by throwsters, a section of the silk industry, to replace the diminishing demand for the throwing or twisting of silk. The British Man-made Fibres Federation lists thirteen brand names of these yarns, each having its special features.

Yarn produced by the spinner is termed a 'singles' yarn; a 'doubled' or 'manifold' yarn is produced by another processer, the doubler, by twisting two or more singles yarns together. Some complicated manifold yarns are made by further combining several doubled yarns. For example, I have interrupted my writing to untwist a six-cord sewing thread and find that it consists of three doubled yarns twisted together. The reader may interrupt his reading in the same way—he will need a pin, a $5\times$ magnifying glass, and an assistant to lend a finger and thumb. For special purposes even more complicated yarns are produced. The specification of a manifold yarn consists of the tex and twist (direction and amount) of the singles yarns, the number combined at the first stage together with the twist (direction and amount), corresponding data for the second stage, and so on. Folded yarns are stronger, more regular, and smoother than singles; sometimes they are 'gassed', i.e., passed through a flame or over an electrically heated element to singe off protruding fibres and make the yarns smoother; sometimes they are mercerized (see pp. 44–5) to make them more lustrous; and sewing threads are waxed and polished. Apart from their use in sewing threads, manifold yarns have mostly industrial uses as in tyre fabrics and conveyor belts. Before the extensive use of man-made fibres, doubled yarns were much used for producing cotton cloths of high quality—poplin shirtings are an example. A poplin shirting made of fine, gassed, and mercerized doubled yarns of Sea Island cotton is a luxury cloth. This kind of use has declined.

The industry produces a wide range of fancy yarns. Flecks of coloured fibres or of other foreign matter can be introduced at an early stage of spinning and so become distributed along the yarn to give a decorative effect. Slubs, or short thick places, can be artificially introduced at spinning, care being taken to ensure that they do not form a discernible pattern. Yarns of different colours may be doubled together to form a 'grandrelle' yarn with the appearance of a barber's pole. By adjusting the rates of feed of the components in doubling, one yarn can be spiralled around the other, or if one is highly twisted it can be made to form small protruding snarls or loops. The variety of effect that can be produced in these and other ways is very large. Most fancy yarns are produced by specialist doublers.

It is only necessary to mention dyed yarns. The production of cloths woven with coloured stripes and checks is only possible if coloured yarns are available.

'Core' yarns, which are produced by the spinner, are composite yarns in which the core is of one fibre, usually continuous filament, and the outside is of another. For example, a 'stretch' yarn of reasonable cost can be made in this way by having as a core one of the very expensive elastomer fibres and on the outside cotton, which provides most of the bulk.

CLOTH STRUCTURES

The cloths produced by the Lancashire industry are woven, as opposed to those produced by knitting or the newer methods of fibre assembly. A woven cloth consists of two sets of interlaced yarns: the warp, the yarns of which extend lengthways along a piece of cloth, and the weft ('filling' in the U.S.A. and 'woof' in poetry), the yarns of which extend across the width.

General characteristics of a woven cloth are that it is relatively inextensible warp-way and weft-way, and that the yarns can swivel at the points of intersection so that the cloth can be distorted in a diagonal direction to a degree that depends on the closeness of the structure. The first of these characteristics influences the draping quality and stability of the cloth, and the second enables it to be moulded over curved surfaces without puckering—a feature that is useful in the making of well-fitting garments. The properties of a particular cloth are affected by, among other things, the tex of the warp and weft yarns, the closeness with which the yarns are set (the threads per inch), and the pattern by which they are interwoven (the weave).

The simplest pattern is the plain weave (p. 39, Fig. 1a), in which each warp thread passes alternately over and under successive weft threads, and vice versa. If the warp and weft yarns have the same tex and setting, the cloth is 'square'. Such a cloth can be thin and open like a gauze, or thin and close (almost paper-like) like a tracing cloth, or thick and close like some canvases. If the warp yarns are more closely set than the weft, say with twice as many to the inch, the warp tends to wrap around the weft which lies almost straight, and the cloth becomes almost warp faced with a weft-way rib. Such in cotton is a poplin and in a filament man-made fibre a taffeta (with a faint rib) or a poult (with a more pronounced rib). If the rib is made very pronounced by having a coarser weft than warp the cloth is a repp. Each of these cloths has a characteristic feel and appearance or sheen.

Weaves of the next simplest type are the twills, of which one is represented in Fig. 1b. There, each weft thread passes successively over two warp threads, under two, and so on, and vice versa; and the order is such as to give a pronounced diagonal rib—the twill line. This is a '2 and 2' twill. In a '2 and 1' twill, the weft may pass successively over one warp thread, under two, over one, and so on; the warp will then pass under one weft thread, over two, and so on, to

---

Plate 4. On the left is a bale of cotton, the covers and steel bands having been removed. In the centre is a partly unrolled lap. On the right are two cans of sliver.
Plate 5. On the left are three bobbins of roving, of different tex numbers. Towards the right bobbins of ring yarn are standing up and two mule cops are lying down. On the extreme right is a cone of yarn that has been wound after spinning.

give a cloth with a less prominent twill line, with warp predominating on one side and weft on the other. Such, and not the garment for a teenager into which some of the cloth is made, is what the textile man understands by a jean. If, say, the warp is coarser and more closely set than the weft, the side on which the warp predominates will have a well-defined texture and will form the 'face' of the cloth.

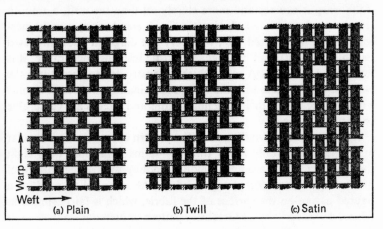

Warp →
Weft →

(a) Plain   (b) Twill   (c) Satin

Fig. 1. Examples of the three basic weaves.

A denim is such a twill, often 3 and 1 with a dyed warp and an undyed weft which gives a speckled appearance on the face of the fabric. In a twill the direction of the rib may be diagonally upwards or downwards from left to right (viewed as this page is viewed), or it may be alternately upwards and downwards over narrow widths to give a 'herring-bone' twill. Twill cloths are looser and more flexible than plain cloths with the same yarns and set, but the construction permits coarser yarns to be woven with a closer set, i.e., to be more tightly packed, than is possible with a plain weave; and so twill cloths can be heavy and compact, and yet flexible. Hence they are suitable for protective clothing such as overalls and, as gaberdines, for rain-coats.

Next after twills in complication come satins in which the 'floats', as the lengths of one yarn passing over successive threads of the other

---

Plate 6. Bale cotton being fed into bale breakers. The output from the breakers is taken by the trunking over the machines into a common trunk for transmission to the next process.
Plate 7. A full lap being removed from a scutcher.

D

are called, are longer than the floats over two or three threads so far described, and are distributed so as to break up the tendency to form a twill line. Fig. 1c illustrates a 5-end satin ('end' is the term used for a single warp thread)—one in which the floats pass over four threads of the other yarn giving a repeat of the pattern every five threads. In the cloth illustrated the warp predominates on the exposed side, and if the warp is coarser and more closely set than the weft, a smooth texture can be achieved. A Venetian is an 8-end satin, usually mercerized and schreinered (i.e., with very fine diagonal lines embossed on it in finishing), and has a characteristic lustrous appearance; it is used for coat linings. A satin which is constructed to accentuate the weft, making the side with the weft predominating the face, is termed a sateen. Because of their long floats satins and sateens are vulnerable to damage in wear.

In plain, twill, and satin weaves the pattern of interlacing is regular and repeats over only a few threads—satins with more than eight threads on a repeat are uncommon. In dobby weaves the pattern of interlacing is more complicated and can be arranged to produce a figured design on the surface of the fabric, which is fairly simple as figured designs go—say, a Greek key pattern or diamond-shaped spots distributed over the cloth. The repeat can be over several inches of cloth.

The designer of jacquard cloths (J. M. Jacquard was the early-nineteenth-century French inventor of the mechanism for weaving them) has more freedom. Every thread within a width of about six inches is separately controlled, and within this width and over a length of a foot or more the interlacings can be controlled almost at will to produce the elaborate 'picture' designs familiar in brocades. The designer's freedom is limited somewhat by technical considerations such as the undesirability of having very long floats.

Honeycomb weaves (the cells of the honeycomb are rectangular) and the like give the cloth thickness and softness and are thus suitable for towels. A more pronounced effect is achieved in terry towelling, which has loops of special warp threads fed into the cloth during weaving.

Cloths with cut pile, such as velvets, are made either by weaving a compound cloth with long floats superimposed on a ground, which are cut in finishing, or by weaving two thicknesses of cloth together and incorporating threads which pass between the two and bind them; the binding threads are cut by a traversing knife at the loom to form the pile.

Very heavy cloths such as are used for conveyor-belts are made by weaving several thicknesses at the same time, and simultaneously weaving in warp threads which bind the layers together.

Net-like (e.g. marquisettes) or cellular cloths can be woven by a 'leno' weave, which involves intermittently twisting adjacent warp threads together, and so preventing the sparsely spaced threads from slipping about in the cloth. These are useful where openness is required without weight, as for heat insulation (the air locked in the large interstices of such a cloth provides the insulation) or in net curtains. A comparatively recent development has been the use of such cloths in cotton for blankets in hospitals, where their ability to stand up to steam sterilization is a great advantage. There are subtleties in the design of such cloths, and not all that look cellular are equally effective for heat insulation.

The 'palette' of the cloth designer is also enlarged by the possibility of combining in stripes yarns of different colours, fibres, and other characteristics. The stripes may be warp-way, weft-way, or (in checks and ginghams) both ways; they may be simple or complex in pattern and may be combined with any weave. The cockled or puckered texture of seersuckers can be produced in weaving by feeding into the cloth different sets of warp yarns at different tensions.

For manufacturing and commercial purposes cloths are specified precisely by their constructional particulars, but many types that have long been articles of commerce have acquired names. Some of these are generally familiar and have entered into everyday language, some are familiar only to people in the trade, some have largely passed out of use. To those already mentioned may be added the following and many others: muslin (after Mussolo in Mesopotamia), calico (after Calicut), cambric (after Cambrai), limbric, scrim, mull, osnaburg, Florentine drill, organdie, voile, pongee, zephyr, corduroy, fustian.

Weaving is the oldest method of making cloths. It is versatile and prolific in the variety of its products and for some uses woven cloths have essential properties that cannot be readily provided by other cloths. Weaving will continue in use for a very long time.

Of the competing methods warp knitting seems to be making the greatest inroads into the markets for woven cloths. It has been estimated that whereas 72 per cent of apparel cloth was produced by weaving and 6 per cent by warp knitting in 1955, the corresponding figures were 58 and 17 in 1965, and in 1975 they will be about equal at 33 per cent.[1] (Weft-knitted and unconventional non-woven cloths make up the 100 per cent.) For warp knitting a warp is prepared as for weaving and the threads are joined by looping adjacent ones together rather than by binding with a weft, but the cloth can be made to have many of the characteristics of a woven cloth. The range of cloths so far produced is small and they have mostly been of man-made fibres; but with experience the range must increase. Some weaving firms have a few warp-knitting machines, but the process is not becoming a part of the Lancashire industry.

Much inventive effort has been directed towards making 'cloths' of fibres assembled in sheets and bonded by an adhesive, or of films, and a few products have succeeded. Cloths made in these ways are likely to compete with woven cloths only in a very few fields unless very considerable developments occur.

Possibly more significant for weavers are developments in assembling yarns into cloths by methods which may be described as combinations of weaving and stitching, or weaving and knitting. Machines for doing this are becoming available, particularly from Eastern Europe, and the development seems promising. How the weaving section of the Lancashire industry reacts remains to be seen.

FINISHES

Some cloth is used in the state in which it comes from the loom, described as 'loom state' or 'grey', perhaps being given a simple brushing or cropping treatment to remove specks, loose pieces of yarn, protruding fibre, and other unwanted matter. But most is subjected to finishing treatments which it receives in works belonging to a distinct section of the industry. There are many treatments which may be used singly or in combination to add to the variety of the products of the industry.

The oldest and most basic treatment is preparation and bleaching. Loom-state cloth contains a size consisting largely of an adhesive which has been added to the warp to facilitate weaving; in addition, if the fibre is cotton there are natural impurities which give the cloth its unattractive, unbleached, 'grey' appearance: these have to be removed. A cotton cloth may be singed by being passed over a gas flame or an electrically heated element (the process carries a sub-

---

[1] D. Brunnschweiler, 'Design and technological innovation in textiles', *The Textile Institute and Industry*, 5, Manchester, 1967, p. 20.

stantial fire risk) to eliminate hairiness, steeped in an enzyme to make the starch in the size soluble, boiled in a solution of caustic soda to solubilize fats and waxes, washed, treated with a weak acid, and washed again. This will remove most of the impurities, but if a clean whiteness is required, it may be steeped in a bleaching liquor before being treated with the weak acid. The traditional bleaching substance is sodium hypochlorite, as supplied to the domestic consumer in bottles at a high price, and the process has to be carefully controlled to avoid damage to the fibre. More recently methods based on the use of hydrogen peroxide and sodium chlorite have gained ground, particularly for bleaching cloths containing cotton and man-made fibre. Sometimes 'brightness is added to whiteness' by dyeing with a fluorescent white dye, a procedure which is of dubious respectability to some old-fashioned technologists.

The preparation of a cloth of man-made fibre is simpler. Bleaching is unnecessary: since the size used for weaving is usually soluble, washing in a warm soap solution is sufficient. The vulnerability of cloths of man-made fibres to marking and damage makes gentle treatment in finishing a necessity.

The simplest way of dyeing cellulosic fibres (cotton and rayon) is by 'direct' dyes, in which the colour is mixed in water and the cloth is impregnated and dried, somewhat after the manner of home dyeing. Compared with the results achieved with other types of dye-stuff, 'direct' colours are prone to fading in light, to rubbing off in wear, and to washing off in laundering, or (in the technologist's language) they are not very fast to light, rubbing, or washing, and so have a limited usefulness. The dyestuffs industry has produced dyes that are fast and have a wide range of colours, the oldest established being 'vat' dyes. Dyeing with these involves impregnating the cloth with the dyestuff in a soluble (or 'reduced') form and then oxidizing it so that the dye is deposited in its insoluble form. Recently technologists have developed so-called 'reactive' dyes, which react chemically with the cellulose molecule so that they become an intrinsic part of the molecule and the colour is consequently very fast. Very bright shades can be produced with reactive dyestuffs.

The new fibres have presented special dyeing problems since they do not readily absorb the dyestuffs used for other textiles, and dyeing materials and methods have to be developed for them. This takes time and is partly why at the outset cloths made from a new fibre are obtainable in only a limited range of colours.

Cloth that is dyed in the piece has the same colour all over unless different yarns are incorporated, say, as stripes, to produce the cross-dyed effects already mentioned. Printing permits coloured designs to be put on the cloth with very few technical limitations. The dye is applied in a paste with, say, a starch base, either from engraved rollers or through a screen acting rather like a stencil, the paste preventing the dye from flowing over the cloth and blurring the design. Each colour is applied separately and the fixation process follows. A limitation for roller printing is that it is only economical for long runs of cloth, and economy is helped if the design is such that it can be repeated in several combinations of colours so that one set of the very expensive engraved rollers can be used to produce a range of cloths. Screens are much cheaper to produce and screen printing is suitable for short runs. If the warp yarn is printed before weaving, the undyed weft softens the outlines of the design and a shadow print results.

Any cloth that has been given a wet treatment is somewhat cockled and creased, as are unironed garments taken from the domestic wash, and hence every one is 'stentered', usually at a late stage in the finishing sequence. Stentering involves running the moist cloth through a machine in which it is slightly stretched widthways and dried by hot air, so that it emerges smooth and in the form in which it is often supplied to the customer. Cloths of synthetic fibres are 'heat set' in this process, the conditions of heating and stretching being carefully controlled to give the required result.

Calendering usually follows stentering. The process consists in passing the cloth between heavy weighted rollers of steel and compressed cotton, and can have a profound effect on its appearance and handle. Before calendering the cloth may be impregnated with starch or some modern plastic material to give the surface a glaze, the permanence of which depends on the material. Calendering and glazing may be accompanied by the embossing of a design on the surface, as for example in schreinering.

Mercerization, which was invented by John Mercer in 1850 and applies to cotton, involves impregnating the cloth with strong caustic soda, stretching it, and washing it while still under tension. The caustic soda swells the fibres, makes them relatively smooth and round, and gives the cloth a lustre. Cotton yarns can also be mercerized, as they often are for sewing and embroidery cottons. If the cloth is not stretched when impregnated with the caustic soda, the swelling causes the warp and weft yarns to crimp and the cloth shrinks. Then, after finishing, it has a small but useful degree of elasticity. This in essence is the modern 'slack mercerization' process for producing stretch cloths in cotton, the degree of stretch being enough to 'give' to the stretchings that occur when garments are worn ordinarily and to recover sufficiently to retain the shape of the garment, which is described as 'comfort stretch'.

Cloths may be given coatings of linseed oil, rubber, or plastic materials to make them impervious to water or to provide a desirable surface as in leather cloths and oil cloths. Here the fabric is a base for the coating and the process should perhaps be regarded as more than textile finishing.

Cloths may be combined with sheets of other materials by adhesives. A 'foam back' is made by combining a thin light foam of, say, polyurethane, with a cloth. The foam adds bulk and warmth with little weight, but it interferes somewhat with the draping qualities. Another combination is made by sticking aluminium sheet to a cloth. Aluminium is a good reflector of radiant heat as well as light, and when it is combined with a cloth without covering the reflecting surface with some varnish the combination can be used to provide excellent insulation against radiant heat. One process is available for pressing the aluminium around the yarns and punctur-ing it at the interstices, thus making the combined fabric permeable to air and moisture—a good feature in fabrics for clothing. When thinking of the usefulness of cloths for protective clothing we should remember the needs of people who are exposed to and have to work in extreme conditions, as in some industries or in the tropics or arctic regions, or even in outer space, as well as those of the ordinary con-sumer. The design of cloths for such needs is an exacting branch of technology.

Anti-shrink processes in finishing Lancashire's textiles are applied to cotton and viscose rayon. The shrinkage, which is different from that in wool, occurs because, in weaving and finishing, the yarns and cloth are inevitably placed under tension and so stretch, and the yarns and fibres in the dried cloth are in a state of strain. When the cloth absorbs moisture, whether from the atmosphere on a damp day or from the water in laundering, the fibres swell and the yarns readjust their relative positions, the direction of adjustment tending to reduce the strains and so causing the cloth to shrink. When dried the cloth remains shrunk. The fibres do not change in length. On subsequent cycles of wetting and drying the process goes further for up to eight or ten cycles, the amount of shrinkage at each cycle being less than that at the previous one, until ultimately the strains are fully relieved and the cloth is stable. Most of the shrinkage occurs in the first cycle, but the subsequent shrinkage may be quite important —up to 2 or 3 per cent. The phenomenon may be likened in some ways to what occurs when a can of powder is gently and repeatedly tapped and the powder settles to a stable condition, the successive tappings corresponding to the successive wettings and dryings. Viscose fibres swell more than cotton and this can be troublesome even in shrunk cloths—such difficulties are overcome by a resin treatment which reduces swelling. Synthetic fibres do not absorb much water and do not swell so that heat-set cloths made from them do not shrink in this way.

The width to which a cloth is stentered can be controlled to obviate subsequent widthways shrinkage. An anti-shrink process deals with lengthways shrinkage by compressing the cloth, forcing it to take up what is considered to be its final stable length, and compressing the fibres and yarns into minute cockles and crimps to achieve this. The subsequent swellings and contractions then remove these cockles and crimps without further contracting the external dimensions of the cloth. The amount by which the cloth can be compressed can compensate for the shrinkage that occurs only on the first wetting and drying, and any residual shrinkage will be experienced in use by the consumer.

Crease-resist, minimum-care, no-iron, and wash-and-wear finishes, which are so much a feature of the modern cotton and viscose rayon textile scene, involve impregnation of the fibre in the cloth with resins, which have many physico-chemical similarities to the substance of synthetic fibres, and confer on the cotton or rayon a degree of some of their properties. Notable among these properties are an ability to recover from deformations such as are imposed in use and to retain smoothness in the cloth, and a reduction in the tendency to

Plate 8. A general view of a cardroom, with the backs of a row of cards on the right, a line of drawframes up the centre, and speed frames in the background. The drawframes are of traditional type that are beginning to be replaced by modern high-speed machines. The drive from overhead shafting through belts is being superseded by drive from individual electric motors.

Plate 9. Close-up view of sliver issuing from the drafting system of a drawframe. The top one of the front pair of rollers has been removed. The rod being held by the hand may be ignored.

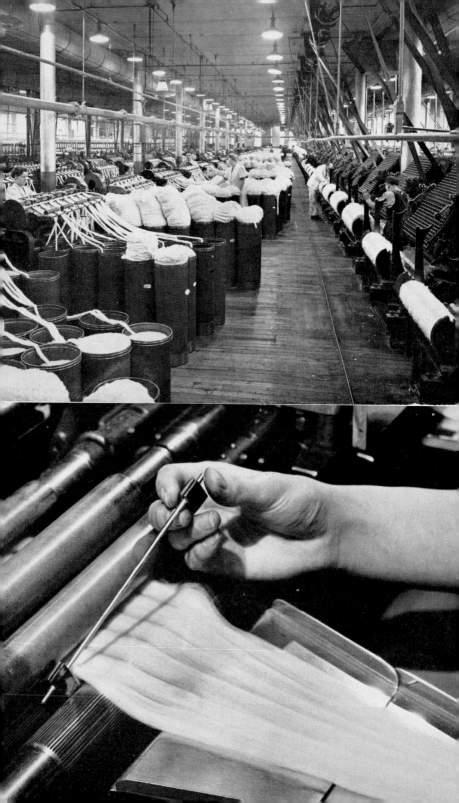

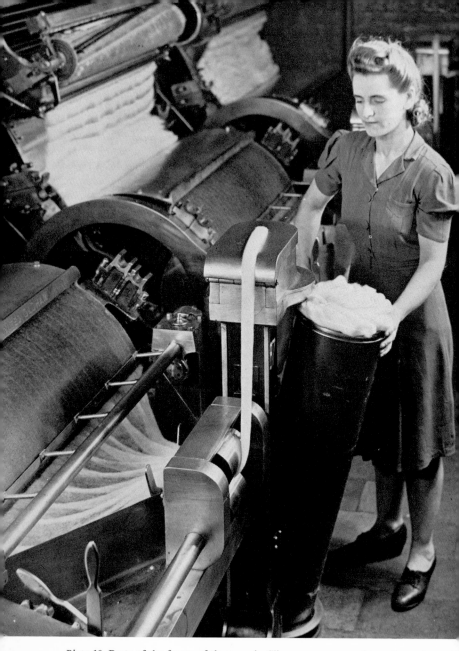

Plate 10. Parts of the fronts of three cards. Sliver emerges as a thin web on the front cylinder. It is seen on the first card being gathered into a sliver. The can in which the sliver has been collected is being removed by the operative.

Plate 11. Slubbing (speed) frames. The foreground shows the back and top of one frame with the slivers passing into the drafting system, which is hidden under the long shelf-like plate. The operative is working at the front of another frame, which shows the slubbing issuing from the front rollers of the drafting system and being wound on to bobbins.

Plate 12. A pair of waste or condenser mules (see pp. 61–2 and 65). These differ from ordinary mules in that the roving is on long horizontal bobbins with about 16 rovings to the bobbin, instead of each roving being on a separate bobbin.

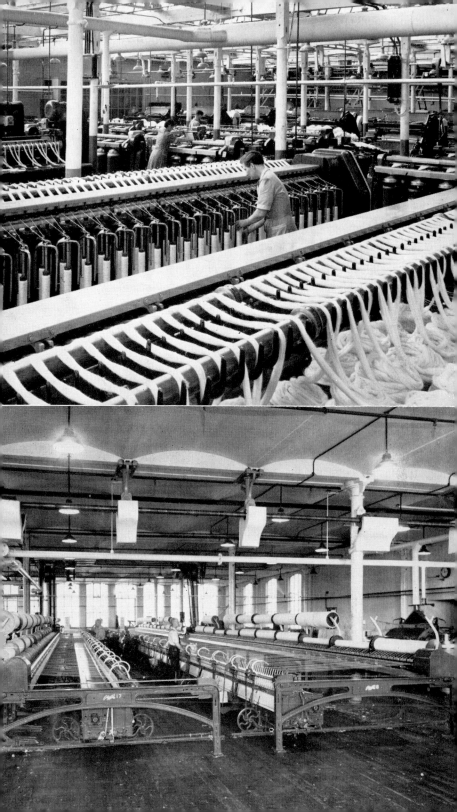

Plate 13. Ring spinning. The black trunk to the left of the spinner traverses the frame and blows air to prevent fluff, or 'fly', from settling on important working parts of the frame.

absorb moisture and swell. Unfortunately the process also reduces the durability of the fibre substantially and to a degree which is roughly proportional to the degree of anti-crease effect achieved. Compromises have to be struck and these vary according to the ideas of the finisher and the uses to which the cloth is to be put. Also, cloths may have to be made stronger and heavier to compensate for the loss in durability—for example the no-iron shirts in the shops today are not made from the fine poplins that were common before the war. Research work is, however, being done on the problem and before long the deleterious effects of the treatment may be reduced or eliminated.

The molecules of a resin used for crease-resisting are too large to be introduced directly into the fibre, and so the smaller molecules of the materials from which it is formed are impregnated, and a subsequent curing or 'polymerization' process forms the resin *in situ*. By a recent development this curing can be postponed until after the garment has been made and pressed, so that its shape (including any pleats) becomes set.

One can think of the crease-resist property being conferred in two ways. One is through the molecules of the resin providing stiffness and elasticity by acting like minute rods; the other is by the molecules attaching themselves at points along the cellulose molecules, so that the whole forms a kind of elastic scaffolding. Which of these two effects predominates is not known.

Raising is applied to cloths of staple yarns, largely of cotton, and is the process of producing a fluffy surface or nap by passing the cloth close to rotating rollers with small wire spikes on them. The spikes engage in some of the fibres and tease them out (it was once done by the action of teasel thistles) to form the short soft pile characteristic of winceyettes and flannelettes. The weft provides the raised fibres and has to be softly twisted. The process is rough and weakens the cloth; careful design of the cloth and control of the raising process are necessary to ensure a satisfactory soft nap without undue weakening.

Much public attention has been devoted to tragedies that arise when cotton garments catch fire—say, nightdresses of children warming themselves before an open fire—and there are now strict regulations on what may be sold. There are several fireproofing treatments possible for cotton but only one is satisfactory in not being irritant to the skin, in not making the cloth harsh, and (above all) in not washing off during laundering. It is used, but unfortunately it is expensive compared with the cost of the cloths on which it is most useful.

A cloth may be made waterproof in two ways. One is by coating it with an impervious film of a material such as rubber to produce a cloth which is thoroughly waterproof but uncomfortable in a garment. The other is to treat it with a substance which (in the language of the physicist) increases the surface tension between air, water, and the textile, so that water does not wet the fibre but runs off exactly like water off a duck's back. These treatments only delay the wetting of the textile and are not suitable for prolonged exposure to rain, particularly to driving rain—hence the term 'shower-proof'. Waterproofing treatments of this kind have been developed to be more effective and durable than they were, and to be suitable for use with the new fibres. Some of them are also stain-resisting finishes.

Cellulosic cloths are prone to attack by micro-organisms if the conditions of use involve exposure to hot, humid atmospheres. Finishing treatments are available for mildew-proofing and rot-proofing tentages and other industrial cloths.

CHAPTER 3

Processes

Filament yarns of man-made fibres are made by the man-made fibre producers outside the Lancashire textile industry (there are some factories for doing this in the geographical county). This section of this chapter is about the manufacture of spun yarn from staple fibre, both natural and man-made. All the processes involved in this are together termed spinning, but the term is also used specifically for the last in the sequence, at which the final yarn is produced. Correspondingly, a spinner can be either (*a*) an employer or the manager of a spinning mill—his full title is master spinner—or (*b*) an operative who works on the final process.

The processes for manufacturing yarn from bale cotton, shown on the left in Plate 4, produce in turn the four types of product illustrated in Plates 4 and 5. The first is a lap (Plate 4, centre), which consists of a roll of soft blanket of partly cleaned and partly opened or fluffed-up fibre. The second is a sliver (Plate 4, right) which consists of a soft untwisted rope of clean fibre coiled into a tall cylindrical container called a 'sliver can'. The third is roving (Plate 5, left) consisting of a soft, slightly twisted yarn wound on to a bobbin. The fourth is the final spun yarn (Plate 5, centre) wound on to a bobbin or in a form known as a 'mule cop'. It will be convenient to divide the description of the processes into four corresponding parts.

Bale to lap. In the cotton-growing country, adjacent to the cotton fields, is the ginnery where the fibre is roughly stripped from the seed in tufts, piled into a baling press, and compressed for transport to the country where it is to be spun. The first processes in the spinning mill are to open the cotton by breaking up the tufts, and lumps into which they have been compressed, and to remove as much dirt and debris as possible, usually about two-thirds of that present. Machines for doing this vary somewhat in principle, but the three to be described are typical.

First the bale is taken to a position behind a bale breaker, where the steel bands and cover are removed, the operative breaking the bands asunder by swinging a woodman's axe against them. The operative takes handfuls or small armfuls from the bale and places them on a travelling lattice which moves intermittently at a creeping speed and takes it into the breaker (Plate 6), where the first stage of opening and cleaning is accomplished. Fibre from the bale breakers is transported pneumatically through trunkings to another room where it is fed on to another lattice which takes it into an opener. This is often coupled directly to the last opening and cleaning machine in the sequence, the scutcher (or picker in the U.S.A.), which produces the laps, each weighing about 40 pounds. Plate 7 shows a lap being removed from a scutcher. Readers who wish to see how these machines work may study Figs 2 and 3. Each machine in the sequence is intended to break up the mass of cotton into progressively smaller tufts, of course without damaging the fibre, and to remove more and more dirt. Elaborate and long sequences were once common, according to the ideas of particular technologists, but as technical knowledge became more profound machines were improved, the number in a sequence was reduced, and results became more certain. The sequence was usually broken at one or more points and this involved corresponding manhandling of the material, but now the machines are linked into a single-opening line so that between being put on the breaker lattice from the bale and being taken from the scutcher as a lap the cotton is not handled. These developments occurred largely between the two wars. Machines for automatically feeding cotton from the bale to the breakers have been developed, but they are not much used. They do not save much labour and have difficulties and limitations associated with them. Automatic machines for removing laps from the scutcher are available and are being adopted more and more.

In addition to opening and cleaning the fibre the bale-lap processes have two functions that are important for the quality of the yarn. One is blending. Even after he has selected cotton as far as is technically and commercially practicable, the spinner has to use material that varies from bale to bale, particularly between bales belonging to different deliveries to the mill made at different times. But he aims to produce yarn of quality that is uniform, in spite of the fact that the production flow in the mill is such that yarn being spun on different spindles at one time may have originated from cotton that was

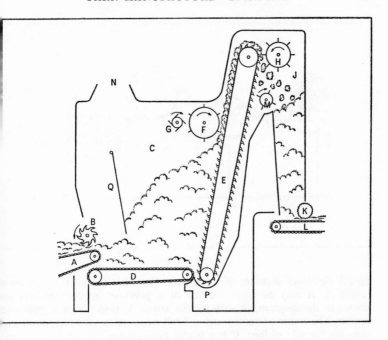

Fig. 2. Sectional diagram of a cotton opener. Cotton on the travelling lattice A is taken into the chamber C by the spiked roller B. Cotton in the chamber C is carried forward by the lattice D to the inclined spiked lattice E which moves continuously, picking tufts out of the mass and carrying them upwards. The rotating roller F, which has leather flaps on it, knocks all but a thin layer of tufts back into the chamber C, the thin layer being carried on by E to the top and over. G is a small roller which clears away any tufts adhering to F. The tufts are knocked from the lattice E by the roller H and fall into the tall compartment J, whence they emerge on the lattice L and under the roller K. The feed to the compartment J is faster than the rate at which the cotton is removed by K and L, so that J is always full, and the overflow is knocked back towards the inclined lattice by the roller M, and finds its way back to the chamber C. The action of the lattice E and the various rollers tends to break up large lumps of cotton into tufts, and this and the tossing about liberates dust which is extracted through the opening N. There may be a grid under the lowest point of the inclined lattice E at P through which heavy dirt falls. In order to maintain a fairly constant feed the flap Q actuates the feed lattice A and roller B when the chamber C needs replenishment and stops them when C is adequately charged. The lattices and rollers extend over the full width of the machine, and the load of cotton at each stage is fairly uniform over the width. This and the constancy of the head in the compartment J ensures that the sheet of fibre emerging at KL is fairly uniform in thickness.

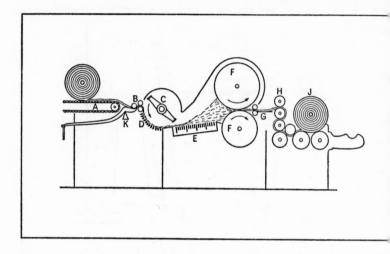

Fig. 3. Sectional diagram of a scutcher. Cotton is fed on the travelling lattice A. It may be from the lap of a previous opener-scutcher, as shown in the diagram, or may be the lattice L (Fig. 2) of a previous opener. The cotton passes through a 3-roller feed system B which positively controls the rate of feed. C is a beater consisting of two steel blades extending the width of the machine on supporting arms that rotate at high speed in the direction of the arrow. As the blade passes the rollers B it knocks off fairly small tufts of cotton, which are taken in an air current over grids D and E through which heavy pieces of dirt fall. F are cages consisting of hollow cylinders of perforated metal through which air is drawn by a fan. The fibres are drawn on to the cages and carried between them; at the nip they are lightly pressed into a blanket which is drawn off between a pair of rollers G. Dust is exhausted through the perforations in the cages. The blanket is compacted by being passed through a system of heavily weighted rollers H and is wound on to the lap J. The lever system fulcrumed at K measures the thickness of the cotton feed under the first roller at B and operates a control system to compensate for variations in thickness at B and produce a more or less constant final lap thickness. This is an early example of an automatic control.

delivered to the mill days or even weeks apart. He pursues his aim by blending the cotton from many bales to secure uniform average quality in the bales. Up to 50 bales may be blended in one mixing, and I have heard of mixings of 100 or more bales. Cotton from several bales is often fed to one bale breaker, and since the mixing that occurs in the machine is not great, a good deal depends on the conscientiousness of the operative in regularly feeding fairly small lumps in turn from the bales. I have heard that in an emergency at one mill, older women were employed for this job instead of the normal men operatives, and that quality improved because the women could handle only small lumps from the bale whereas the men were apt to feed the material in large armfuls. Further blending is achieved by combining the output from several bale breakers, as seems to be done in the mill illustrated in Plate 6. The traditional breaks in the opening and cleaning sequence already referred to were used to provide additional opportunities for blending. For example, laps from an opener-scutcher would be combined in fours to feed the finisher scutcher. Another method, 'stack mixing', has been abandoned because it is too costly. Altogether, the modern labour-saving developments in opening and cleaning processes have reduced the amount of blending, and sometimes mills run into trouble in consequence. However, methods of restoring a degree of blending are being tried and methods of selecting bales are being improved.

A second important function is producing laps that have a uniform weight per unit length (tex) both within and between laps. The subsequent processes reduce the tex successively in definite ratios to produce the yarn of the ultimate tex, and variations in tex in the lap are transmitted (with modification) to the yarn. The first rough control, which is self-acting, is at the outlet of the opener (at KL in Fig. 2). The second, automatic and more refined but still crude, is at the regulating mechanism of the scutcher (Fig. 3). The third is manual and is achieved in the following way. The length of blanket forming the final lap is automatically controlled to a constant value by a measuring and stopping mechanism working from the front rollers, so that if the weight of the lap is constant so also is the tex. Each lap is weighed; those that are too far from the required weight are rejected (they are reprocessed), and at intervals the operative adjusts the scutcher to correct for persistent errors in weight. A 'closed loop' regulating device for measuring the thickness of the lap between two of the front rollers (H in Fig. 3) and making corrections automatically has been invented, but has not so far been much adopted.

To the extent that the processing has been successful, the laps are of fairly clean and opened cotton, well blended from many bales, and of fairly uniform tex. Laps of man-made fibres are made in much the same way as of cotton except that the cleaning and blending are less elaborate.

Lap to sliver. The lap is made into a sliver on a card, the main functions of which are to complete the opening, i.e., to separate the fibres from each other, to almost complete the cleaning and removal of very short fibre, to reduce the tex of the product to about one-hundredth of that of the lap, and to produce a very slightly compacted sliver. Plate 8 shows on the right the backs of a row of cards, with partly used laps feeding into them, and Plate 10 shows parts of the fronts of three cards, with sliver issuing from the first and being collected in a can, which is being removed by the operative. The operation of the card is explained in the legends to Figs 4 and 5.

Full laps are brought to the cards by male operatives, who are usually assisted in their work by some form of mechanical conveyor. Women card 'tenters', as the operatives who attend to the running of machines in the spinning mill are termed, remove the full cans, taking them to a convenient position for the next process, and effect the necessary repair when occasionally the sliver breaks before it enters the can. The maintenance of the cards, with the critical close settings of their parts and the cleaning of the cylinders, is skilled work performed by men known as strippers and grinders.

Carding has remained fundamentally unchanged for many decades, but during the past few there have been labour-saving developments in details. The cans into which the sliver is coiled have been made larger and now hold five or six times as much sliver as they did, so that each time an operative moves a can she moves that much more material. This development started before World War II but its application has since been extended to practically all mills, and cans are now as large and heavy as the tenters can handle. Cans of the two commonly used sizes, old and new, are shown in Plate 4.

Since the early 1960s carding speed, i.e., the rate at which sliver is produced, has been spectacularly increased so that now speeds of up to five times those formerly used are quite common. Increasing the speed does not of itself reduce labour, but it reduces the capital for new labour-saving equipment for a given output and so helps with

Plate 14. Cone winding machine. The bobbins and cones are on a travelling 'belt' so that as they pass the operative and knotting head, breaks, etc., are attended to In the background are the creels of beaming machines (see Plate 15).
Plate 15. The beaming of a striped warp. Cones of yarn that feed the machine are contained in a creel.

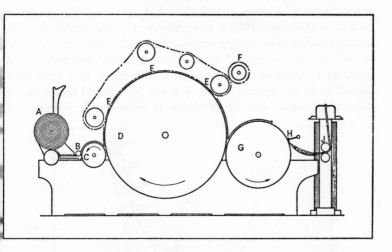

Fig. 4. Sectional view of card. Material from the lap A is drawn forward at slow speed under the driven roller B. C is a fastly-rotating cylinder with vicious saw-toothed spikes on it which comb the fringe of fibres being fed forwards by B, and draws them in an air stream under C towards the large cylinder D. Heavy dirt falls out of the air stream and through a grid. D is thickly covered with wire spikes and as it rotates it takes up the fibres from the air stream and carries them under the 'flats' E. These consist of flat bars extending across the width of the card, mounted on an endless chain, shown by a broken line, which moves very slowly so as to change the flats over the cylinder D. The side of the flats facing the cylinder is thickly covered with fine wire spikes which are set with a gap of only a few thousandths of an inch between them and the spikes on the cylinder. The fibres on the cylinder, which are very sparsely distributed over it, are combed by the spikes on the flats and the result is that foreign matter and tangled fibre are taken by the flats and the fibre remaining on the cylinder is cleaned. As the flats move away from the cylinder they come under the rotating brush F which cleans them, the material removed being utilized by waste spinners. G is a rotating cylinder thickly covered with wire spikes, called the doffer. Fibre from the main cylinder is taken on to the underside of the doffer and at H is removed by a vibrating comb extending across the width of the card. The thin sheet of fibre (it looks almost like a cloud) is then gathered to form a sliver, which is calendered under the rollers J and then coiled into the can. The ratio of the speed of output at J to the speed of feed at B is the ratio in which the tex of the lap is reduced to form the sliver. The fast-moving cylinders cause a strong and complicated air stream

---

Plate 16. Tape frame seen from the creel of warper's beams.
Plate 17. Tape frame, with sized yarn being wound on to a weaver's beam.

E

the economics of development. The history of carding speeds is curious. Until about 1960 it was received doctrine that for a high-quality product slow carding was essential, and spinners would boast of the slowness of their carding. Then, a heretic had the idea of speeding up carding, with technical modifications that have since proved to be unimportant, and so it has been found that sliver of acceptable quality can be produced at high speed, without any

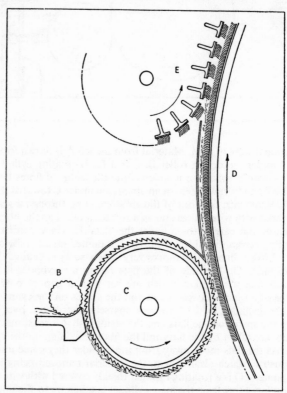

Fig. 5. Enlarged sectional view of the back of the card. B is the feed roller, C the saw-toothed 'taker-in', D the main cylinder with wire spikes on it, and E are flats. The surface speed of the flats is very slow compared with that of the main cylinder.

within the card and this plays some part in the transfer of fibres from one cylinder to another, although exactly how is not fully understood. Fig. 5 gives an enlarged view of the feeding end (the back) of the card.

fundamental change to the process. The whole attitude of mind of spinners has changed. High-speed carding has its problems, but they are as much problems of management and engineering as of textile technology.

Another modern development is the feeding of cotton from the scutcher directly to the cards through trunks and chutes, without the intervening formation of laps. This necessitates some control of tex (usually automatic) to replace that normally achieved by weighing laps. Chute-feeding of cards is now a practical proposition but is likely to be adopted only in new installations incorporating also other new developments.

After carding, the sliver is passed to the drawframe where it is subject to drawing. Six or eight card slivers are fed to one unit (a 'delivery') of the drawframe, where they are combined to produce one drawframe sliver of approximately the same tex as that of one card sliver. The process is described in the legend to Fig. 6 (p. 58). Banks of drawframes and card sliver feeding them occupy most of Plate 8.

The drawframes perform two functions. The fibres in a card sliver are hooked, crinkled, and higgledy-piggledy, whereas for spinning they require to be straight and parallel, and the achievement of this is one function. One drawing is not enough so there are two or three in series (they are termed 'heads' of drawing). Sliver is collected in cans from the first head and passed to the second where it is further drawn, and so on. Because of the crudity of the controls up to carding—the control through lap-weight is the last so far—card slivers vary in tex. The averaging effect of combining them at the drawframe reduces the variation in the product, and so performs the second function of drawing. For example, if each drawframe delivery is fed with six slivers and there are two heads, each finisher sliver will contain parts of $6 \times 6 = 36$ card slivers and will hence be much more uniform than the single card slivers. The combination is termed 'doubling'. If there are three heads of drawing there will be $6 \times 6 \times 6 = 216$ doublings of card sliver. Doubling also helps blending. Unfortunately, although doubling reduces the variation from sliver to sliver, the associated drafting increases the variation along the length of the individual slivers.

Since finisher sliver is relatively regular from sliver to sliver the finisher drawframe is used as a control point for the tex of the product. Periodically, say, once or twice a shift, measured lengths of sliver are weighed to estimate their tex, and if this is not at the required value the machines are adjusted. Adjustments are necessary only very infrequently.

The drawframe tenter is usually a woman, who doffs full cans of

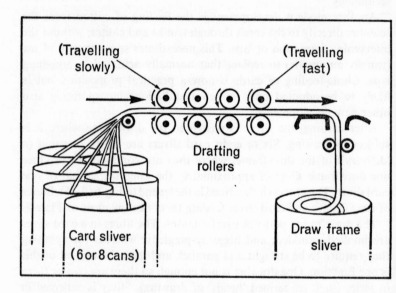

Fig. 6. The principles af drawing and drafting. Slivers from six or eight cans are passed over a guide roller and then between four pairs of drafting rollers, not unlike the rollers of a domestic mangle but smaller. The three distances between the centres of the pairs of rollers are slightly greater than the length of the longest fibres, and the two rollers of each pair are pressed together so that fibre cannot slip between them. The back rollers rotate slowly and the other pairs progressively more quickly until the front pair move about six or eight times as fast as the back pair, so that the issuing drawframe sliver has approximately the same tex as one card sliver. It is coiled into a can. The action of the rollers is to draw the fibres forward faster than they are being fed, so causing them to slide over each other and tending to straighten them. There are four pairs of rollers in the drafting system because it is necessary to achieve the six- or eightfold draft in stages.

Plate 9 gives a close-up view of the drafting system of a drawframe with the front top roller removed. There are several sets of rollers, or 'deliveries', on one drawframe; the complete one nearest the camera in Plate 8 has four.

If only one sliver is fed, the tex of the issuing sliver is one-sixth or one-eighth of that of the sliver fed, and so a degree of attenuation, or drafting, is achieved. The principle of this method is used later in the processes of spinning.

sliver, transfers them to the next head or to a position from which they are taken to the next process, and joins the full cans of supply sliver to the feed. She also makes a repair when the sliver breaks.

The first development from the traditional system, which occurred largely between the two wars, was the reduction to two heads of drawing. Previously three were thought to be necessary, and in some mills that strove after very high quality four were used. Two heads, with the corresponding saving in labour, gives a product that meets modern requirements, provided modern standards are applied in the processing.

The second development is the use of larger cans. The story is the same as that already told for cards. One new drawframe has cans which hold 100 pounds of sliver.

The third is the adoption of high-speed drawframes. Speeds of up to 1,500 feet per minute are used and of 800–1,000 f.p.m. are common, compared with the traditional 150 f.p.m. The new frames are better engineering products than the old, and have improved drafting systems, and so produce better sliver. The chief significance of high speed is in reducing the amount of machinery that has to be bought in adopting the large cans, and in reducing the number of points where process control has to be exercised.

The most modern development is the so-called 'automation' of the production of finisher sliver, for which several systems have been devised. Generally they involve feeding the cards from the scutcher through chutes and linking cards and drawframes so that material is fed continuously from the one to the other or, alternatively, adopting some automatic system of transfer. There is usually some modification of the drawing, and automatic means for controlling tex are required. With these systems the cotton is not handled between being put on the breaker lattice from the bale and sliver being removed from the drawframe. 'Automated' systems are being operated in a few mills in different parts of the world (Japan is a pioneer in this field), but so far they must be regarded as experimental and it is too soon to say what shape automation will take in the spinning mill. There is not much saving in labour as compared with the little labour required to produce sliver on a modern set-up of conventional kind, and the automatic equipment is so expensive that there is little or no saving in cost. The chief advantage is probably in the resulting freedom from dependence on the human element in the maintenance of quality.

Sliver to roving. Although sliver can be spun directly into yarn, most is first spun into a roving. This is performed on a speed frame, of which two are shown in Plate 11. Single slivers are taken into the frame where they are attenuated by a roller drafting system not unlike that used on a drawframe, and the issuing roving is wound on to bobbins. While being so wound it is given a slight twist to give it sufficient cohesion to withstand the tensions imposed in further processing. Sliver, being thick, has sufficient cohesion without twist; the thinner roving needs twist but is not given enough to cause the fibres to break when the roving is attenuated in later processing. The functions of the speed frame are thus to attenuate the material fed to it and to package it in a form suitable for later processing.

The duties of the women speed frame tenters are to piece new material into the feed when a sliver can runs out, to doff the full bobbins and replace them by empty ones, and to effect a repair when the roving breaks in processing.

Traditionally there were three sets of speed frames in series, each producing a slightly finer roving than it receives from the previous one. The first is called the slubber, and its product slubbing; the second is the intermediate frame or inter, and its product is inter roving; the third is the roving frame proper. At the inter, two slubbings are usually fed to give additional doubling. Slubbing and inter are merely coarse rovings. In some mills producing fine yarns there would be four speed frames, the last being the jack frame.

These many processes and the corresponding labour requirement were necessary because with the roller drafting systems and machinery available the product would become unduly irregular in thickness if too much drafting were done in one stage. A draft of four or five was about as much as could be safely achieved. New systems, termed 'high-draft' systems ('long-draft' in the U.S.A.), were invented and the precision to which they were manufactured was improved, so that the draft could be increased. With modern systems drafts of ten are common at speed frames, and of twenty or more at spinning. Thus the number of speed frame processes could be reduced. They were reduced to two where medium and fairly fine yarns, and to one where coarse yarns, are spun. Exceptionally yarn is spun in one stage directly from sliver.

The other modern development in the speed frame processes has been the use of larger bobbins to increase the productivity of the operatives who handle them.

Roving to yarn—Spinning. Spinning consists in attenuating the roving (or, in direct spinning, the sliver) to the tex required in the yarn, inserting the twist that gives the yarn its strength, and winding the yarn on to a former or bobbin. The attenuation is done by a drafting system which has been developed from the roller system to make high drafting possible. There are two methods used in Lancashire for performing the other two functions: mule spinning (on a machine called a mule) and ring spinning (on a ring frame).

The mule is about 125 feet wide (or long, depending on the viewpoint) with several hundred spindles (say, 900–1,300) on it, able to spin as many threads of yarn at the same time. It consists of a creel to contain the hundreds of rovings at the back, the drafting system just in front of the creel, and a 'carriage' containing the spindles on to which the yarn is wound. The carriage is many yards wide (or long) and is mounted on wheels so that it can move towards and away from the creel and drafting system over a distance of a little over five feet. These features may be seen in Plate 12.

Mule spinning is an intermittent process. The carriage starts near the creel, and as it withdraws attenuated roving is delivered so that at the end of the run there is about five feet of it between the tip of each spindle and the drafting rollers. All this while the spindles are rotating to twist the attenuated roving and form yarn (see Fig. 7). Then, after a complicated manœuvre known as 'backing-off', the carriage reverses direction and runs inwards to the drafting rollers

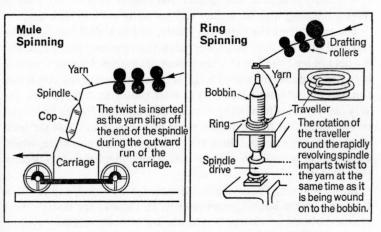

Fig. 7. The principles of mule and ring spinning.

while the spindles continue to rotate and the yarn is guided so that it winds on them to form the cop (two cops are lying on their sides in Plate 5). The cycle, which takes about 15 seconds, is then repeated until, after some hours, the cop is full. The mules are set in pairs as shown in Plate 12 so that on their outward run the carriages move towards each other until there is only a narrow space between them. The space in which the operatives work is known as the 'wheel-gate'. It is impressive to see the wide carriages majestically moving to and fro (rather like a line of soldiers on parade), with spindles whirring, and the thousands of spinning threads being displayed. The sequence of operations is controlled by a complicated mechanism consisting largely of belts or ropes and pulleys, which is a monument to Victorian engineering ingenuity.

A pair of mules is run by a team of men operatives, usually a spinner or minder, a big piecer, and a little piecer. Their duties are to replenish the roving when it runs out, doff full cops, mend threads broken during spinning (this is skilfully done during the first few feet of the outward run of the carriage), and keep the mules clean and in good operating condition. The minder, who is a skilled man, also controls the mechanism. The little piecer is an apprentice and the big piecer is a more experienced man who formerly would expect to become a minder (the decline in mule spinning denies him that opportunity). This traditional arrangement of labour is modified slightly in special circumstances, even to the extent of the help of women being occasionally accepted. The minder and piecers have to move about during spinning with fair agility and normally work in bare feet.

The mule treats the yarn very gently, and in skilled hands can be made to produce finer and softer yarns than the ring frame can. But it does not lend itself to modern labour-saving developments such as high drafting and the use of large bobbins, and the mule cop is not suitable for automatic handling in later processes. The demand for very fine yarns is diminishing or vanishing, and ring frames have been so improved that they can spin yarns fine enough to cover the bulk of the industry's needs. These are reasons why in Lancashire, where almost alone it has been used for cotton spinning, the mule is becoming obsolete.

In ring spinning the roving is attenuated and twisted, and the yarn is wound on the bobbin, continuously. In Plate 13 the tenter's head is near bobbins of roving, her hands are near the drafting system, and her knees are near the bobbins of spun yarn. The points at which the yarn is wound on to the bobbins are hidden by vertical guard plates. The principle of ring spinning is explained in Fig. 7. If the spinning is direct from sliver the creel of roving bobbins is replaced by one containing cans of sliver, and it will be seen that it is not easy to make space to accommodate their bulk, even though specially small cans are used. The tex is controlled by weighing measured lengths of yarn and adjusting the machine accordingly. If all the other tex controls are working properly machine adjustments should rarely be necessary after a tex has become established.

Ring frame tenters are usually women. Their job is to join up fresh supplies of roving, mend (or 'piece-up') broken yarn, and keep the frame, particularly the region around the drafting system, clean. Short fibre liberated during spinning (it is termed 'fly') is very troublesome. It floats about in the atmosphere and settles on the machinery. If neglected it gets into the bearings of the drafting rollers and accumulations drop on the yarn and cause bad places. Constantly it has to be wiped away and removed. There are mechanical and pneumatic devices for assisting in this (for example, the black vertical object to the left of Plate 13 is a trunking that traverses the frames and air from it blows fly off the spinning area of the machines) but much remains for the tenter to do. Full bobbins of yarn are doffed by a special gang of males or females, and mechanical adjustments to the frames are made by male ring jobbers.

Modern developments in ring spinning are the invention of high-draft systems and the devices referred to for removing fly; improvements in the engineering precision of the machinery leading to increased speeds and greater regularity in the yarns produced; and the use of large bobbins to save labour in handling, both in spinning and in later processes. In the early post-war years bobbins were made as large as was practicable, but it was discovered that when the size was increased beyond a certain point the extra costs for space and for power to drive the bobbins on the spindles outweighed savings in labour costs, and so optimum bobbin sizes were established and are now generally adopted.

No devices have so far been produced, even for trial in mills, for automatically replenishing the roving supply or mending yarn broken in spinning, and little progress in this direction is likely for many years. The fundamental difficulty is in thinking of automatic devices cheap enough to be fitted to the thousands of spindles in a mill. Progress has, however, been made with automatic doffing devices and mills are likely to adopt them during the next decade or so.

Another development that is in sight, although its application is for the more distant future, is of 'break spinning'. In ring spinning the insertion of twist involves the rotation of the bobbin, and there are limits to the speed with which this can be done—limits which have been substantially reached. Break spinning involves twisting the roving into yarn as it is being drafted without necessitating the rotation of any bobbin. This can be done at exceedingly high speeds, and the yarn can be economically produced on very large bobbins. The development should lead to economies and to yarns with new (and it is to be hoped desirable) qualities. Several devices are in the patent literature, small-scale experiments have shown that they are practicable and promise well, and the production of industrial equipment is beginning.

So great has been the change in the processes of the spinning mill that the labour required to produce a pound of yarn in a modern mill is roughly one-third of what it was between the two wars, or even less. This saving has been produced, as we have seen, largely by using large cans and bobbins and by shortening the processing. Whereas in the typical mill there would formerly be nine points of transfer of material between processes, in the corresponding modern mill there are five. There has been no change in the principles of spinning; a nineteenth-century spinner walking into a modern mill might be astonished but he would not be mystified.

The shortening of the processing has been helped by the invention of new drafting devices, but I think that the most important influence has been the improvement in the precision of the machinery. At least until World War I, and possibly even until World War II, textile machinery was made to the engineering standards of the early parts of this century. For example most of the gear wheels were of uncut cast iron. Master spinners wanted cheap machines, and little was asked of them but that they would work. Technologists did not know how important engineering precision was for the quality of the product. Spinners made the best of the equipment available and produced good yarns by slow processing through many stages with much blending and many doublings, and this involved much handling and the employment of many operatives. An improvement in the quality of the machinery was the only way out of this situation, and the increase in production rates that became possible was, from the point of view of the technologist, a by-product, albeit a valuable one.

Yarn may be delivered from the spinning mill in the form of either spinner's bobbins or mule cops packed in cases or skips, or it may be wound and beamed by one of the processes described in the next section. Usually, however, it is first 'conditioned'. As it comes from the spindle point the yarn is very dry and 'lively' (i.e., inclined to snarl), and a little moisture must be added to facilitate further processing. This was formerly done by standing the yarn over pools of water in the mill cellar for some days, but now measured amounts of water with a wetting agent are sprayed on as the yarn passes through a conditioning machine. The procedure has technical justification, but spinners are not oblivious to the commercial advantages of selling water at the price of yarn, and the whole subject has been a bone of contention between suppliers and customers for generations. The obvious expedient of measuring the moisture in delivered yarn and charging for the dry weight is apparently too direct for commercial use, and conventional moisture allowances are adopted.

Other spinning-related processes. Three processes that are more or less closely associated with spinning will now be mentioned.

Combing is an additional process sometimes inserted in the sequence of drawframes with the object of removing some of the short fibre that is present in the best of cottons and improving the parallelization of fibres in the sliver. It is an expensive process and in Lancashire it is used for yarns of the best quality.

Yarn from waste fibre and low-grade cottons is produced in separate mills on the condenser system. After the opening, laps of fibre are carded twice on condenser cards, which resemble those used for carding wool. The web from the second card is not condensed into a sliver but is split into rovings which are little coarser than the yarn, and are wound on to the long bobbins shown in Plate 12. In spinning the roving is not drafted in a roller system but is stretched slightly during twisting to produce the slight attenuation required. Spinning has been done mostly on mules but in re-equipment schemes specially designed ring frames are being substituted.

Yarn doubling is usually done in special mills. The number of yarns required to be twisted together are wound on to a bobbin or 'cheese', and this is placed in the creel of a frame very like a ring frame. The yarns are fed forward, of course without drafting, and

twisted as they are wound on to the final bobbin in the same way a
yarn is twisted in ring spinning. Twiner doubling is the mule equiva
lent of ring doubling; it was quite common between the wars bu
now has substantially disappeared. Uptwisting, which is used fo
twisting continuous filament yarns, belongs to the throwing sectio
of the silk industry.

PREPARATION OF YARN FOR CLOTH MANUFACTURE

Very little spun yarn can be woven or knitted directly in the form i
which it comes from the spinning spindle, and so it goes throug
preparatory processes which will be described under the thre
headings of winding, beaming, and warp sizing. Parts of thes
processes also apply to filament yarns, but the main description wil
be for spun yarns.

Winding. This is the transfer of yarn from the spinner's bobbin o
cop to a larger package, the most usual form of which is nowaday
the truncated cone to the right in Plate 5. The objects of the proces
are to remove weak places, lumps, and slubs from the yarn, substitu
ting well-tied knots, and to achieve a long continuous length on th
package, so that in later processing yarn will run in long lengths with
few breaks. Whereas there are three or four spinner's bobbins to th
pound of yarn, or even more, a cone weighs one or more pounds.

A cone winding machine such as that shown in Plate 14 has on i
roughly 100 heads. The cone is driven, and draws yarn from th
bobbin through a tensioning device (often a pair of weighted o
spring-loaded discs which apply a frictional drag) and a 'clearer' t
remove lumps and slubs—in its simplest form it consists of two plates
forming a slit little wider than the diameter of normal yarn. When the
spinner's bobbin becomes empty or the yarn breaks, the cone may
continue to rotate or, on some machines, be lifted clear of the drive,
but in any event winding on that head ceases until the operative has
made a repair. Winding can be from mule cops or ring bobbins, but
the former is dying with the mule.

Until World War II, much of the spun yarn in Lancashire was
wound on crudely made, slow-running machines, belonging in
design and often in manufacture to the nineteenth century, which
wound yarn on to relatively small wooden bobbins. These are now
entirely superseded. Modern winding machines, forms of which have
been available since the early years of this century, vary in detail, but

all are precision-built, run at speeds of up to 1,300 yards a minute, and make large packages—usually but not invariably cones. They may be entirely manually operated, or be equipped with various automatic mechanisms to do parts of the work of winding.

On a manually operated machine the operative, a woman called a winder, replenishes the supply of spinner's bobbins by putting the bobbin on the spindle, threading up the tensioning and clearing devices, and joining the new yarn to the old on the cone. She also removes full cones and joins up the yarn to a new former (this needs to be done much less frequently than the first job); and she mends broken threads or 'ends'. Cleaning is done occasionally—say, once or twice a shift. In carrying out her work she patrols the frame and for tying knots she has a mechanical knotter strapped to her hand. Much of her time is spent in replenishing the supply, so that the size of the spinner's bobbin has a predominating influence on her productivity.

Part of this work is made automatic by systems that employ an automatic knotter, which may either patrol the frame in imitation of the operative, or (as in Plate 14) be stationary and the spindles be made to traverse around a circuit while winding and to pass under the knotter in turn. The operatives still have to manipulate the bobbins and cones and place the ends of yarn in convenient positions, but the reduction in work is substantial. Some of the newest machines are so automatic that the operatives pour spinner's bobbins into a hopper and remove empty bobbins in a skip; only the cones are handled individually. It is not practicable to wind from mule cops on any of these newer machines.

A modern development is the use of electronic clearers. These detect thick places and other imperfections by means of a photo-electric 'eye' or a small electrical condenser, without touching the yarn; and they can be made very selective in the type of defect they detect, taking account of length and shape of the defect as well as its thickness. The device breaks the yarn at a defect and the operative effects the repair. Electronic clearers are expensive, but at the high winding speeds now common they are economic.

Some continuous filament yarns of man-made fibres are wound on to cones, but many are supplied by the producers in large packages suitable for further processing without rewinding.

The cone is a good form of supply package for later processes. It can be used directly in knitting, and in beaming for weaving (as will be seen in the next section). If the yarn is softly wound on to perforated formers it can be used in yarn dyeing. It is a good supply for automatic machines for weft winding.

In addition to cone winding, there are other forms of winding. For doubling, two or three or as many yarns as are required to be combined into one, are wound together on to a 'cheese' which is very like a cone but is cylindrical. If yarn is required in hanks, say, for dyeing or for mercerizing, it is wound from spinner's bobbins into hanks, and after processing is wound back on to cones.

Weft winding is necessary because the yarn needs to be on small bobbins or 'pirns' that will go into the shuttle. Traditionally mule cops were used directly in the shuttle without rewinding, and for a time small ring-spun bobbins were also so used. Nowadays practically all weft yarn, whether spun or continuous filament, is wound on to pirns from cones, or from the equivalent package from the producer of man-made fibres. This is done in the weaving mill.

Beaming. As the next stage in its preparation for weaving or warp knitting, warp yarn is wound on to 'warper's beams' by the process of beaming or warping. Plate 15 shows the set-up. Five or six hundred cones are placed in a large creel, and the 500 or 600 'ends' are drawn forward to the beaming frame where they are wound side by side on to a driven cylindrical former with flanges which is the beam. There will be thousands of yards of yarn on a full beam. The lateral positions of the ends are controlled by a comb, and if the warp has coloured stripes the ends are positioned approximately according to the required pattern, as is shown in Plate 15. Each end passes through the detector of a stopping device so that if one breaks the beaming is stopped. Each end also passes through a tensioning device on the creel.

All yarns, whether staple or continuous filament, are beamed in substantially the same way, but with synthetic fibres difficulty sometimes occurs through the generation of static electricity causing the yarns to balloon out or to cling together. This can be obviated by treating the yarn with an 'anti-static' dressing or by the use of a static eliminator, which ionizes the air around the yarn so that the charge can leak away.

The beamer's main job is to watch over the running of the machine, to mend the few broken ends, and to ready the machine when new cones are supplied or a full beam is doffed. Full cones are usually put into the creel by assistants, although the beamer may help. The full beams weigh hundreds of pounds and have to be handled by men with mechanical aids.

Developments over the years have been the substitution of cones (or, in the Barber Colman system, cheeses) for the older wooden bobbins, engineering refinements in the equipment, increasing speeds, and increasing the size of beams. The regularity of yarn tension and thread spacing is all-important for satisfactory weaving or knitting, and attention is paid to this. Magazine creels which permit the installation of new cones during beaming before the old ones have run out, are now commonly used as a means of increasing the productivity of the beaming frame.

Traditionally beaming has been done as much in the weaving as in the spinning mill, but more and more it is becoming the province of the spinner or the supplier of man-made yarns.

Warp sizing. During weaving the warp yarn is subjected to considerable rubbing and tugging and needs the protection of a size, which, for a staple yarn and most filament yarns, is applied in the process known as warp- or tape- or slasher-sizing. A tape frame is shown in Plates 16 and 17. Warper's beams are mounted in a creel at the back of the machine (Plate 16), as many as are required to give the total ends (warp threads) required in the cloth. In Plate 16 there are eight warper's beams, so that if each contains 500 ends there are 4,000 in the cloth. These are drawn forward together and the final sheet passes over a roller at the back of the frame into a 'sow box' containing the boiling size (steam can be seen rising from the box in Plate 16). After the sheet of yarn has passed through the size it is mangled between two rollers to remove the excess size, and passed around two large steam-heated cylinders for drying. On emerging from the drying system the individual threads of the warp, which have become slightly stuck together, are separated by a system of 'splitting-rods', passed through a comb which controls their spacing and the width of the sheet, and wound on to the weaver's beam. This is shown in Plate 17. One 'set' of warper's beams will produce up to about twenty weaver's beams, each of 1,000 yards or more.

The operative in charge, the 'tape sizer' or 'taper', with an assistant, prepares the size mixing and threads up the machine at the beginning of a set, and during sizing he controls the winding of the yarn on the weaver's beam and, through adjusting the speed, the degree of drying. Traditionally he was given a very free hand, his work being judged solely by the performance of the warps on weaving, and he operated the process as an art, or even a mystery. Gradually, as the several processing variables have become understood and made measurable, he has been given prescriptions and his work has been made more scientific. Even in 1920 in some mills the ingredients of the size and their proportions were his secret, and weird and wonderful were some of the mixtures used. Now the mixture is prescribed by the management and usually consists of an adhesive (a starch for cotton, and some easily soluble adhesive for man-made fibres) and a lubricant (usually tallow for cotton, and something more expensive for man-made fibres). The amount of size put on the warp is important because if there is not enough the warp is inadequately protected and if there is too much the yarn is made stiff and harsh; in either event ends break unduly in weaving and cloth quality suffers. Formerly the taper assessed the amount by the uncertain method of feeling the yarn, but now careful attention to the concentration of the mixing and to the method of preparation gives the necessary control. Likewise it is important that the sized yarn should be neither over- nor under-dried, and the taper formerly assessed moisture by 'feel'; now an electrical moisture-measuring instrument guides the sizer and he is instructed as to the reading to which he should work. In a few installations the measuring instrument actuates an automatic speed control. These changes have occurred gradually during the past four or five decades and have had a great effect in improving the weaving quality of the warps produced. The skill of the sizer is still required to ensure that the weaver's beam is uniformly and compactly wound and that the threads lie parallel and uncrossed.

The latest development is to make automatic the preparation of the size mixing and the control of the amount of size put on the warp. This is making its way into the industry.

The system described is that largely used in Lancashire for sizing staple yarns. Other countries and some Lancashire mills adopt methods that differ only in some details, such as the method of drying. Most continuous filament yarn of man-made fibre is sized in substantially the same way as staple yarn, but for some

Plate 18. A Lancashire, or non-automatic, loom (the lettering corresponds to that in Figs. 8 and 9). L are the two staves carrying the healds and R is the top roller through which the up and down motion of the healds is transmitted. K is the reed, M part of the sley which moves to and from the cloth, E is the cloth, G the breast-beam, H the take-up roller, and J the batching roller. PP are two picking-sticks—arms that swing horizontally and through the straps project the shuttle across the loom.

Plate 19. Close-up view of the shuttle starting on its way across the loom. The lettering is as for Plate 18.

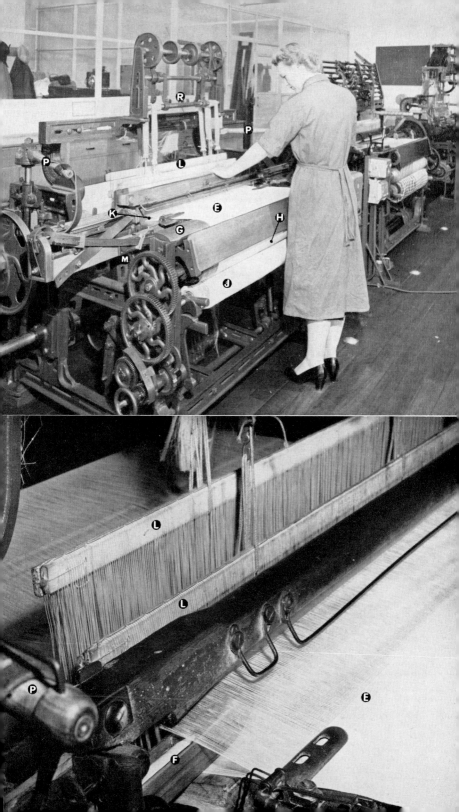

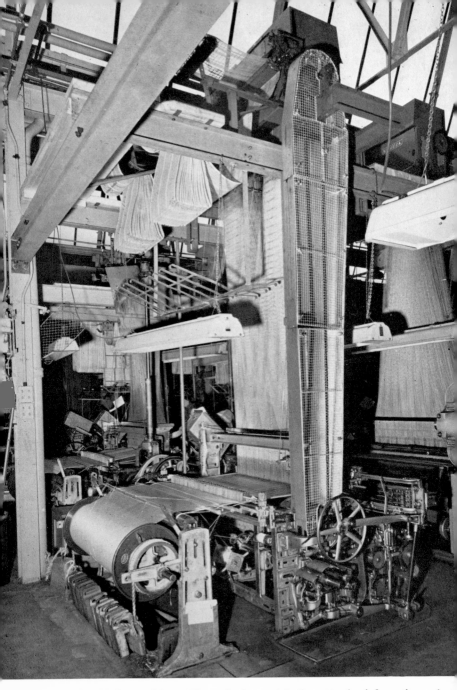

Plate 20. Jacquard loom. The cards that contain the patterning information and the patterning engine are supported by a gantry high overhead. Strings from this engine are connected to the heald eyes at warp level.

of it the system used is substantially that formerly used in the silk industry.

Sizing is mostly done in the weaving mill but a little is done by separate commission sizers.

CLOTH MANUFACTURE—WEAVING

In Lancashire the manufacture of woven cloth from yarn is termed manufacturing without qualification, and the corresponding employer or manager is a manufacturer. Although he is also termed a weaver, that term is usually reserved for the operative at the loom, and weaving usually refers to the process of interlacing yarns to form a cloth. It would be possible to make a woven cloth by darning the weft threads one at a time over and under the warp threads, but this would be very slow and laborious, and quite early in pre-history man seems to have thought of deflecting the warp threads so that the weft could be passed straight between them, over some and under others. This principle of weaving is described in Fig. 8 (p. 72), and the corresponding elements of a loom are in Fig. 9. Plate 18 gives a general view of a Lancashire loom, and Plate 19 a close-up of a shuttle entering the warp at the beginning of a traverse. Readers who are unfamiliar with weaving and the elements of its terminology are recommended to study these if they wish to follow the discussion of this section.

During weaving the picking-stick oscillates to simulate a human arm (Plate 18), projecting the shuttle from one side of the loom to the other, alternating the sides. (The action is termed 'picking' and a 'pick' is either one such action or a weft thread.) Meanwhile, the sley moves towards and away from the cloth and the healds move up and down, the cycle being repeated some 200 times a minute. The sley is away from the cloth when the healds are separated to allow for the passage of the shuttle. The whole process is noisy and, to the newcomer, intimidating. Most of the noise comes from the impacts involved in the rapid and frequent starting and stopping of the shuttle. The rapid and frequent stretching of the warp as the healds rise and fall and the crossing over of the ends in the two sets of healds constitute the rough treatment that necessitates sizing.

The loom of Plate 18 is weaving a plain cloth; one weaving a twill or satin would differ in having three or more sets of heald staves, according to the weave. A loom weaving a dobby cloth would have

F

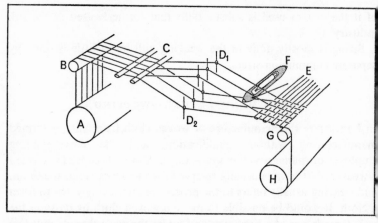

Fig. 8. The principles of plain weaving. Warp yarn from the weaver's beam A passes over the back-rest B of the loom, past lease-rods C which ensure that the order of the threads is maintained, through the eyes of the healds D_1 and D_2. At E, the 'fell', the cloth is formed by the insertion of the weft trailing from the shuttle F. The cloth passes over the 'breast-beam' G and is wound on to the cloth roller H. The shuttle moves to and fro and the interlacing is achieved by raising the D_1 set of healds and lowering the D_2 set when the shuttle moves in one direction, as shown, and lowering D_1 and raising D_2 when it moves in the opposite direction.

even more sets of healds and a mechanism, either over the top of the loom or at the side, for producing the pattern by controlling the order in which the heald staves are lifted and lowered. On a jacquard loom the healds are not on staves but are tied to separate strings which are attached to the patterning mechanism high above the loom (see Plate 20). If there are several colours in the weft there are a shuttle for each and a 'weft mixing motion' for changing the shuttles automatically according to the required pattern. For weaving special fabrics such as one with a pile there are two beams mounted one above the other at the back of the loom.

The loom shown in Plate 18 is termed an overpick loom because the picking arm moves over the loom, in a horizontal plane. The overpick mechanism is characteristic of the Lancashire non-automatic loom, now being superseded. On modern underpick looms the picking arm is a lever pivoted at the base of the loom and moving in a vertical plane (Plate 20). The difference between the two types is largely one of engineering convenience but it does affect the appearance of the loom.

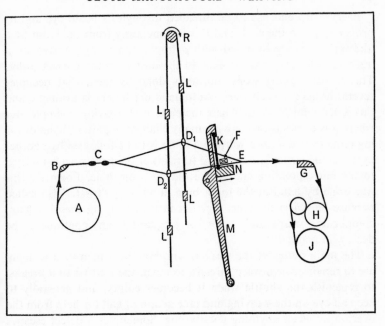

Fig. 9. The elements of a loom (the lettering corresponds to that in Fig. 8).
A is the weaver's beam, B the back-rest, C are the lease-rods, and D the
eyelets of the healds. The healds are on shafts L which move up and down,
being (for a plain weave) actuated by treadles worked by cams under the
loom, the movement being transmitted from one stave to the other over
the oscillating top-roller R. E is the fell of the cloth, and F is the shuttle.
When the healds are raised and lowered, the yarns form a V-shaped tunnel
with the apex at E, through which the shuttle passes. It passes over the
bottom sheet of warp threads which are constrained by a wooden guide N,
or 'race-board', attached to the sley M; and it passes in front of the reed
K. The reed is essentially a comb, extending across the width of the loom,
and supported in the framework of the sley. Its vertical teeth pass between
the warp threads, and control the spacing accurately. After the shuttle has
completed its traverse and is out of the way, while the healds are reversing
position for the next weft insertion (or pick), the sley M, which is pivoted
at its base, is driven by a crank towards the cloth, and the reed K pushes
the trail of weft that has just been left by the shuttle home to the fell—it
'beats up' the weft. This while, a mechanism drives the take-up roller H
so that it moves the cloth forward by the distance between two weft threads
in the cloth. The cycle is then repeated with the front healds down and the
back healds up, and the shuttle moving in the opposite direction. J is a
batching roller on to which the cloth is wound.

Every warp end has to be threaded through its heald eye and its proper space in the reed, and this is done away from the loom by a 'drawer', working by hand with a hook, and being assisted by a 'reacher' who presents the ends to the drawer in the correct order. This is painstaking work, normally done by men, that occupies several hours for each warp. Automatic machinery is available and this is economical to use where the pattern of weaving is simple, but where it is complex or there are many changes in pattern hand drawing remains in use. If a warp in a loom is to be followed by another of the same particulars each end (thread) of the new warp is knotted to the corresponding end of the old by a machine. Formerly this was done by hand at the loom by a 'loomer' or 'twister' (so called because he twists the ends together instead of tying them). Again, complicated warps and warps for jacquard looms continue to be dealt with manually.

The main duties of the weaver, who may be a man or a woman, are to repair broken warp threads, to repair the weft when it breaks, to replenish the shuttle when it becomes empty, and generally to keep an eye on the weaving and take action or call for help from the overlooker when anything goes wrong. Sometimes a defect escapes immediate attention, and the weaver may have to unweave a few inches of cloth—a lengthy and troublesome business. Fresh warps are installed in the loom and 'gaited', and the looms are set and maintained in working order, by overlookers or, in the local slang, 'tacklers'. Traditionally each overlooker attends to all these duties, but in some mills they are divided among specialists—warp gaiters, fitters, and overlookers proper. Most of the jobs have to be done while the loom is stopped, and further production is lost when looms have to await their turn for attention because the weaver is busy. The percentage of its time for which the loom runs on average, the 'loom efficiency', is an important index of productivity that is closely watched by the management. A reasonably good efficiency on non-automatic looms is about 80 per cent and on automatic looms it is between 90 and 95 per cent.

The improvement in the precision of manufacture that has occurred for all textile machinery has been very important for looms. The traditional Lancashire loom was a 'blacksmith's job', made almost entirely from rough castings, filed to make them fit. As yarns have become more regular and greater uniformity in the cloth has been required, so it has been found necessary to improve the loom.

For example, if there are irregularities and eccentricities in the train of gears driving the take-up roller (this train is seen clearly in Plate 18), the picks (weft threads) are irregularly spaced and under certain conditions this produces unsightly weft-way streaks in the cloth. Hence as a first step the old cast gear wheels were replaced by machine-cut gears, and later the whole design and manufacture were improved. Other mechanical features are equally important. These problems became acute in the late 1920s when the regular lustrous yarns of continuous filament rayon first began to be woven, and even looms traditionally used for weaving silk had to be improved. Nowadays looms are assembled from machined castings, and those for weaving continuous filament yarns of man-made fibres are of high engineering quality—and cost. Associated with these improvements are increases in loom speed—increases of up to 30 per cent have been achieved for conventional looms.

Another improvement, as important as any change in machinery, has been a change in the character and effectiveness of the overlooker's work. The setting of traditional looms and rectification when things went wrong was an art, in the exercise of which the overlooker used unsystematized experience, and was guided by the senses of sight, hearing, and feel, the whole sometimes being apparently tinctured with a touch of mysticism. He had, for example, to cope with the flight of the shuttle without the ability to distinguish clearly between velocity, momentum, acceleration, and force. Now all that has changed and is changing. Research has analysed and measured the loom factors that affect weaving performance and cloth quality; essential measuring instruments and gauges have been devised and the improved precision of looms has made their use feasible; and technical education is transmitting the knowledge to the men in the mill.

The replenishment of the weft in the shuttle is a large part of the weaver's work on Lancashire looms, and this depends on the size of the shuttle and of the cop or pirn of weft that it can contain—the greater the length of yarn on the pirn the less being the work of replenishment. During the 1920s and 1930s, weft 'package' sizes were increased as far as practicable. Mule cops were at the time used directly as weft, and were increased in size so that they weighed up to ten or twelve to the pound instead of the former twenty to thirty. The direct use of ring-spun yarn was tried but did not long survive because the length of yarn that could be spun on to the bobbins was too small. Pirns of rewound yarn were made as large as practicable.

And larger shuttles were used to contain the larger packages. These changes caused the 'more looms per weaver' movement of the inter-war years.

However, there are limits to the practicable size of shuttle, and hence to the length of yarn that can be contained, imposed by limits to the extent to which the healds can be moved without unduly stretching the warp yarn and by considerations of weight. The first development to circumvent these was to render the work of replenishing the weft automatic. This, and only this, is the essential feature of the automatic loom contrasted with the non-automatic or Lancashire loom. In the operation of an automatic loom weft pirns are placed in a creel or 'battery' by a 'battery filler', and when the shuttle needs replenishment a full pirn is fed into place and the empty one ejected in the short pause when the shuttle reverses direction at the end of a pick, so that the loom as a whole does not stop. This is good for cloth quality because it is difficult to stop and restart a loom without producing a weft-way mark, which may be quite pronounced if the yarn is continuous filament. The ability to achieve this is one of the special skills of the weaver.

The automatic loom as described has been in use since the beginning of the century, but there have been two post-war developments. One is a 'box loader' to replace the battery, which is loaded automatically at the pirn-winding machine. The other is a winding spindle attached to the loom, which winds pirns from cones and automatically transfers them to the shuttle as required. Only the cones have to be handled.

Many inventions have been made of looms in which the weft is fed directly from a large stationary cone or other package, without being wound on to a pirn, thus avoiding the problem of weft replenishment. This involves cutting the weft at every pick or alternate pick so that special devices are necessary to bind the weft at the edges of the cloth and form selvedges. 'Selvedge motions' are an essential part of any such loom. These looms are becoming economically advantageous with the current trends towards wide cloths and coarse wefts. In such cases the capacity of a conventional pirn is sufficient for only thirty seconds of weaving time, and the high rate of changing overloads the pirn-change mechanism of even the most modern automatic looms of conventional type.

These new types of loom use several methods for sending the weft across. One is to project a small shuttle-like gripper which carries the pick of weft. This is the method used on the highly successful Sulzer loom, which was developed and is made by the Swiss firm Sulzer, and is being installed fairly extensively in Lancashire. The loom is outstanding in its originality and in the excellence of its design and manufacture, features which the firm epitomize in their publicity by going back to linguistic first principles and calling it a 'weaving machine'.

Other methods of weft projection or carrying involve (a) positively controlled arms or 'rapiers' which move in and out along the path normally taken by the shuttle or (b) an air jet which puffs the weft thread across or (c) a water jet which does the same thing. Commercial models of all these types are in use, but so far not to any appreciable extent in Lancashire. When first introduced, almost all new types of loom are suitable for only a limited range of cloths and conditions and are economic only in limited circumstances. As time goes on some limitations are overcome and the loom becomes more generally useful.

All these developments affect only weft replenishment. The repair of breaks in the yarns remains to be done by the weaver, and the only way of reducing loom stops for this, and the corresponding work and effect on cloth quality, is by improving process control. There are warp-break detectors which stop the loom when a break occurs. These have been available for decades and are fitted to non-automatic as well as automatic looms.

Woven cloth is taken from the loom and passed over a machine where it is inspected for defects and 'plaited' (i.e., laid into one-yard folds), ready to be bundled for transfer to the warehouse or finisher. Minor defects are rectified, but major defects, which cannot be entirely avoided, are marked by 'strings' sewn into the selvedge so that they can be readily detected in later processing and, in due course, cut out.

FINISHING

There are many more finishing processes than there are finishes, and they are used in different combinations according to the cloth, the result required, and the equipment and ideas of the finisher. In order to give an impression of how finishing is operated and to introduce some of the machines, a particular sequence will be described, which may or may not be exactly like one operated in any particular mill, but is similar to that operated in many in Lancashire.

The sequence is to bleach and calender a sheeting. The cloth comes from the loom in 'pieces' of about 100 yards and these are first stitched end to end to form a long batch. It is passed in 'open width' through a singeing machine, and then through a pad mangle where it is impregnated or 'padded' with an enzyme preparation.

A pad mangle consists of a trough containing the liquid and two or more mangle rollers, rather like those on a domestic mangle but larger. The cloth is passed through the liquid and through the nip of the rollers so that it carries forward enough of the liquid to make it feel damp. This machine is much used in finishing for padding enzymes, starch mixtures, resins, dyes, and so on. The amount of liquid left in the cloth depends on its viscosity and on the roller particulars —the nature of their surface and the pressure between them—and control of this quantity is often important.

After being padded with enzyme our sheeting is roughly piled or plaited into box trucks and allowed to stand overnight while the enzyme works on the starch. The soluble matter is then washed off in a wash mangle, which is like a pad mangle in principle except that the trough contains water which is continually changing. The cloth is loosely gathered into a rope form for washing. Plate 21 shows it passing through a circular porcelain guide into an old-fashioned wash mangle.

Then the cloth, still in rope form, is piled in a kier, which is rather like a very large pressure-saucepan, large enough to hold one or two tons of cloth. Here it is boiled under pressure for about ten hours (except for the pressure the process is reminiscent of the boiling our grandmothers gave to clothes in the old-fashioned 'copper') in a solution of caustic soda. Then it is washed, and piled into a cistern where sodium hypochlorite is circulated through it for two hours. It is again rope-washed and then piled into a second cistern where a dilute mineral acid is circulated through it. It is further washed thoroughly. After all this the cloth has become bleached, but is still in the rope form and is very wet. It is opened on a scutcher (not the scutcher of the spinning mill), excess water is squeezed off by a mangle, and the cloth is dried on steam-heated drying cylinders (a set is

Plate 21. Bleach croft with cloth in 'rope' form passing through a circular guide into a washing mangle of traditional type.
Plate 22. Cloth passing over drying cylinders and entering a stenter on the left.

Plate 23. The end of a modern continuous bleaching range. Cloth is leaving a mangle on the left, passing over drying cylinders, and passing through a stenter on the right. It is treated in 'open width' (as opposed to rope form) throughout.

Plate 24. A dye jig. Cloth passes from one roller to the other through the trough containing the dye liquor.

Plate 25. Roller printing. Only one roller is in position, but brackets for three more rollers (to apply different colours) can be seen.

shown in Plate 22), and plaited on to trucks for transfer to the next stage in finishing—finishing proper, bleaching being regarded as preparation for finishing.

Our sheeting will be stentered and calendered. It is padded with a starch preparation, partially dried over steam-heated cylinders, and passed into the stenter—this could be what is happening in Plate 22, where the cloth is moving from right to left. On the left it is seen entering the clips of the stenter which grip it at the selvedges and carry it into the machine, stretching it widthways the while. It enters a chamber where hot air is blown on it to complete the drying and set the cloth at its width, and (in this instance) is collected in plaited form on trucks. There is a view of another, modern, stenter to the right of Plate 23 showing the chamber (here the cloth is moving from left to right).

After having been stentered, our sheeting is slightly damped (much as the housewife damps linen for ironing) and calendered. A calender consists of heavy rollers pressed strongly together, around and between which the fabric passes. The rollers have slightly resilient surfaces whose deformation at the nip smoothes as well as presses the cloth. The choice of roller materials (wood, compressed paper, and steel are variously used) and pressures determines the finish attained.

Pad mangles, wash mangles, drying cylinders, stenters, and heated chambers are also used in connection with other finishes, most of which involve applying some liquid preparation, inducing a chemical reaction, and so on, but some items of equipment are specific to particular finishes, and will now be mentioned.

Dyeing liquors are commonly applied by a jig such as that illustrated in Plate 24. This consists of a tank containing the liquor and two driven rollers on to which cloth can be wound. It passes from one roller, through the liquor, and on to the other until the first is empty. Then the motion is reversed and the cloth goes from the second roller to the first. This is repeated until the cloth has taken enough dye material from the liquor. It is then taken to other machines for developing, fixing, washing, drying, stentering, and so on.

The raising machine has already been mentioned in Chapter 2 (p. 47).

Plate 26. Screen printing by hand.
Plate 27. Ace and Rugby mills at Chadderton.

Compressive shrinking is done on a machine that uses something like the following principle. If a thick rubber belt has first a circular path, say, round part of a roller, and then comes off to a straight path, the surface of the rubber is stretched over the circular and relaxed over the straight path. If cloth is brought on to the rubber surface at some point in the circular path and is pressed against it until after the straight part has been reached, the rubber will carry the cloth with it as it relaxes, and so force the cloth into a slightly shorter length. The application of heat during the process sets the cloth in its shortened or 'compressed' state.

Most printing of cloth is done by machine- or roller-printing, as illustrated in Plate 25. The design is put on a roller by fine grooves being engraved where the printing paste is required to be held and left smooth where it is not, the circumference of the roller being equal to the repeat of the design. There is a roller for each colour. Associated with each is a trough containing the colour paste, and a roller rotating in this transfers paste to the printing roller. An accurately made and set blade, a 'doctor knife', scrapes the paste from the surface of the printing roller, leaving it only in the fine grooves, and from there it is printed on to the cloth against which the printing roller presses. Plate 25 shows the machine with one roller-trough system in position, but brackets for three further systems can be seen. The printed cloth, which is moving upwards in the picture, is dried and taken to other processes for the developing and fixing of the colour and so on. The colour paste is supplied to the troughs by apparently primitive hand methods from buckets. The paste must be of such consistency that it properly fills the engraved grooves, comes away from the smooth parts of the roller, transfers itself to the cloth, and does not run on the cloth before drying.

To be economical roller printing requires long runs of cloth with the same design. Greater variety and scope in design can be achieved by the more expensive process of screen printing, shown in Plate 26. A screen is a fine net made of silk or a man-made fibre, through which dye can permeate to the cloth beneath. A pattern is put on the screen in some impermeable material so that the whole acts like a stencil. There is a screen for each colour and the colours are applied successively. The printed cloth has to be finished in the usual way. Plate 26 was taken a few years ago, and as portrayed the process is performed by hand; now it has been largely mechanized.

The methods described involve processing cloth in batches, with
orage and transfer at many places between stages. Modern develop-
ents are in the direction of linking processes so that they can be run
ontinuously, continuous bleaching being an example. Plate 23
ows the finishing end of a modern continuous bleaching range,
ith mangle, drying cylinders, and stenter in series. These develop-
ents raise two requirements. First, chemical reactions have to be
eeded up so that they are completed while the cloth is passing
rough the machines. For example, the overnight storage of our
nzyme-padded sheeting and the ten or more hours in the kier must
e avoided. This involves choosing suitable reactions (for example
leaching with hydrogen peroxide instead of hypochlorite), and
ometimes raising the temperature. Second, some provision has to be
ade for delaying the progress of the cloth through the machines at
arious stages so that time is given for the reactions, even though
ey are accelerated, to take place. This is done by inserting in the
ne a J-box, which is a large box having a section shaped like a
ollow letter J and extending across the width of the machine. Cloth
nters at the top of the J and leaves at the bottom, and in between
nough is contained, being roughly rucked up, so that about half an
our elapses between its entry and leaving, when the process is run
t full speed. Continuous processing saves labour and cost where
here are very long runs of one type of product, and this often obtains
n bleaching. Where variety in product is required, as it must be in
uch of finishing, batch processing is inevitable, although com-
romises are adopted and there are 'semi-continuous' ranges.

CHAPTER 4

Mills, Works, Firms, and the Industry

Except for the occasional enlargement or modification of existing buildings there has been substantially no new building of spinning mills since the early years following World War I. The typical spinning mill is a long, five- or six-storied building, often architecturally aggressive and with the mill name proudly blazoned on the chimney or tower (Plates 27, 29, and 40), usually of brick; some of the earlier ones (mostly those belonging to the nineteenth century) are modest buildings of stone. With their chimneys they give the spinning districts their characteristic appearance, and with their many windows make a fine sight, especially when lit up at night and seen from some hillside across a valley. Most of the mills in the Oldham and Rochdale areas are impersonal, having special, usually short names: Ace, Ash, Kent, Lilac, Majestic, Manor, Mons, Wye. These are frequently the names of the original spinning companies. Some of these mills have been known locally by the name of the founder. In other districts the original company was more often named after the people who founded it, and the mills are also so named: Eckersley's, Wolfenden, Greenhalgh and Shaw, Harwood, Wright.

Until recently the drive was by steam engine, and one necessity was a mill pond or 'lodge' containing cooling water (Plate 27), unless the mill was on the banks of a canal. To distribute the drive there would be one or two shafts along each storey, ending in a pulley and ropes from the pulleys would be driven from the fly-wheel of the engine. The engine house of Ace mill is the building with rounded windows in Plate 27; the rope race joins it to the main building, and pulleys at the ends of the shafts are in the unwindowed near corner of the mill. The engine room was always kept spick and span, with polished brasses and steel, and the hum of the flywheel and ropes conveyed an impression of the power and speed of the drive. The rope speed was close to the Board of Trade maximum of 110 feet a econd—roughly 75 miles an hour. Plate 28 shows a mill engine, probably the last in Lancashire, that was taken out of service in 1966. Nowadays most of the machinery in the mill is driven by electric motors either attached to the individual machines or driving groups through belting and shafting.

Mostly, the lowest floors of the mill are devoted to the warehousing of raw cotton and yarn, and to the opening and cleaning processes. The view of a corner of an opening room in Plate 6 is fairly typical, except that more people are shown than are employed on so few machines, and the floor has been cleaned up for the photographer. It is good housekeeping not to have pieces of cotton lying about on the floor, but few mills can maintain the high standard of cleanliness shown in Plate 6 all the time.

Above the opening and cleaning department comes the cardroom, which contains the cards, combers (if any), drawframes, and speed frames, and is operated as a single department; Plate 8 shows a general view of one. In this mill the cards are driven by belts, probably from a group electric drive. The long sausage-like thing under the ceiling is a fabric trunking which filters the air supplied to the room by the ventilating system and eliminates coarse particles of dust and fibre.

On entering a cardroom one's first impressions are of a pleasantly warm dry place, which only becomes uncomfortably hot on some summer days. If the machinery is pre-World War II there is a trying high-pitched skirling noise that comes from the speed frames, each spindle of which is driven by a cast gear. Modern machines have cut helical or plastic gears, and since there are also fewer spindles installed, modern cardrooms have a comfortably low level of noise.

If long staple cotton or man-made fibre is being processed the atmosphere is acceptably clean, but if medium or short staple cotton is being processed it is (or was) rendered uncomfortable by the short fibre ('fly') and fine dust floating about, which sticks to the hair and clothing. The dust is more than uncomfortable because operatives who have been exposed to it for some years are liable to the disease of byssinosis which in bad cases is lethal; even exposure for a few months produces discernible effects. 'Dust in cardrooms' has been treated as a serious problem in Lancashire for about half a century. Most of the harmful dust originates from the cards, and until recently it has been found impracticable to enclose them because frequent access is required to work them. During the 1950s, the

Shirley Institute developed a successful system for extracting dus
laden air from the cards. This is now installed in many mills, an
with its availability (and the availability of other similar devices) th
Factory Inspectorate is able to insist on a good standard of atmo
pheric cleanliness in cardrooms. Cardrooms are now more comfor
able and pleasant than they were, but unfortunately some of th
harmful dust may evade the extraction system and it is not certai
that they are safe. Chemical and medical research is being directe
to the discovery of what is the very elusive element in cardroom du
that causes byssinosis, and the progress that is being made giv
hope that the medical problem will be solved before long.

Traditionally the cardroom is run in parallel lines, terme
'preparations', each of which consists of a complete sequence fro
cards to roving frames and is self-contained. For example, sixtee
cards may feed a set of eight drawframe deliveries which in turn fee
a slubbing frame, and this may feed two or three roving frames (
there are so many processes). The production at the different stag
is balanced so that the whole preparation works continuously an
there is substantially no storage of material between the processe
The machines are arranged compactly and conveniently to facilita
the transfer of material, much of which is still advantageously dor
by hand carrying and by the sliding of cans of sliver over the floor.
large mill can have twelve preparations, each of which can process
different mixing of fibres. One embarrassment against which ste
have to be taken is sometimes the contamination of the material o
one preparation by fibres floating over the air from another. Chan
ing the mixing or tex on any one preparation is a major operatio
that can be undertaken only occasionally. Mostly, each tenter look
after one frame or group of frames, and does all that is required t
keep them running.

One of the headaches in operating an integrated sequence c
processes arises from absenteeism. The absence of one key operativ
can stop a whole preparation, or badly affect its running, particular
if the other operatives are so heavily loaded with duties (as they ten
to be in an efficient set-up) that they cannot do the extra required t
fill the gap left by the absentee. At times and in some mills the almo
daily rearrangement of the operatives in such a situation has been
serious part of the supervisor's work.

The pattern of working described, varied in detail according t
circumstances, has been in use in Lancashire for generations. Whe

tempts were made to improve the efficiency of the industry by
deployment in the mills after World War II, new patterns were
ied, particularly by breaking down the work of the tenters among
ecialists. Although these attempts have doubtless left some mark,
bstantially the traditional pattern has persisted. The adoption of
e newest high-speed cards and drawframes and of automatic
stems will create entirely new situations.

Exceptionally, ring spinning frames are integrated into the
quence following the cards and are housed in the same room, but
ostly they are in a separate department, in the floor or floors above
e card room. Rovings are taken in trucks up the hoist to the ring
om, and rovings from any preparation may at different times go to
fferent ring frames. It is not a long job to change the tex on the
ng frames so that a variety of yarns can be spun, although the less
e variety and the greater the continuity the better is it for economy.
here is substantially no storage of rovings between the two depart-
ents and the manager tries to arrange that the average tex of the
rns spun and sold is such that a balance is maintained between the
rd and spinning rooms.

The ring room is a pleasant, reasonably quiet place. Most modern
ills have replaced old mules and ring frames by a smaller number
f high-production ring frames, and consequently ample space is
vailable (Plate 30). 'Fly' is something of a nuisance that is being
ealt with and so far no health hazards have shown themselves in
ng rooms.

One hazard of the past is mule spinners' cancer. This came from
e oil used for lubricating the spindles, which rubbed on to the
inners' clothing and skin. The risk of cancer was reduced, if not
iminated, by the adoption of non-carcinogenic oils.

One feature of the cotton spinning mill is the way in which in the
ter stages of processing the package (bobbin, etc.) sizes decrease
nd the number of producing units (deliveries on the drawframe and
indles on the speed and ring frames) increases. For example one
t of drawframes with eight deliveries may ultimately feed a few
ousands of ring spindles. As a consequence, more labour is often
mployed in the ring room than in all the rest of the mill. This feature
lso limits the extent to which automation can be economically
dopted at the later stages, as we have seen (pp. 63–4).

The need for damp atmospheric conditions for cotton spinning is
uch exaggerated in the popular mind. Very dry conditions cause

difficulty, but mills produce quite happily with relative humidities c
45 or 50 per cent, and these are by no means damp conditions
Constancy of atmospheric conditions is more important, and som
mills have conditioning plants to achieve this. Most important of a
is cleanliness of the air in the workrooms, and in industrial Lanca
shire, especially on a foggy day, this can only be reliably achieved b
having an expensive air-filtering plant.

Winding and beaming are usually done on the top floor of the mil
Again, this is a pleasant, quiet room, but the use of high-spee
machinery is beginning to increase the amount of 'fly' in the atmos
phere, and make things unpleasant if not unhealthy. The problem i
not very difficult and is receiving attention.

Doubling is sometimes done in a separate department of a spinnin
mill, but mostly it is done in a separate mill which, in genera
atmosphere and appearance, is not unlike a small spinning mill.

A mill that spins waste fibre is usually small. It is often an old an
somewhat rambling building, made of stone, and tucked away ii
some corner of the Rossendale Valley or of a neighbouring town.

WEAVING MILLS

The heart, and main extent, of the weaving mill is the weaving she
(or, in the U.S.A., weave room), which is single-storied and almos
always has saw-toothed roof lights. Associated with it are rooms fo
winding and beaming, sizing, twisting and drawing, cloth examin
ation, and cloth storage; these may be single- or multi-storie
annexes (Plate 31). Sheds are of stone or brick according the locality
Since the war there has been more new building for weaving than fo
spinning. Existing sheds have been refloored and renovated, and on
or two new sheds have been built. The latest idea imported from th
U.S.A. is to have a building without windows to help the mainten
ance of a constant conditioned atmosphere, the lighting being entirel
artificial. There is at least one shed of this kind in Lancashire. Th
drive was formerly by steam engine, but now electric drive is almos
universal, each loom and machine usually having its own individua
motor.

The first impression on entering the weaving shed is of the noise
The noise level varies from shed to shed according to the concentra
tion and type of machinery, but with orthodox fly-shuttle looms it i
always uncomfortably high and often is probably high enough t

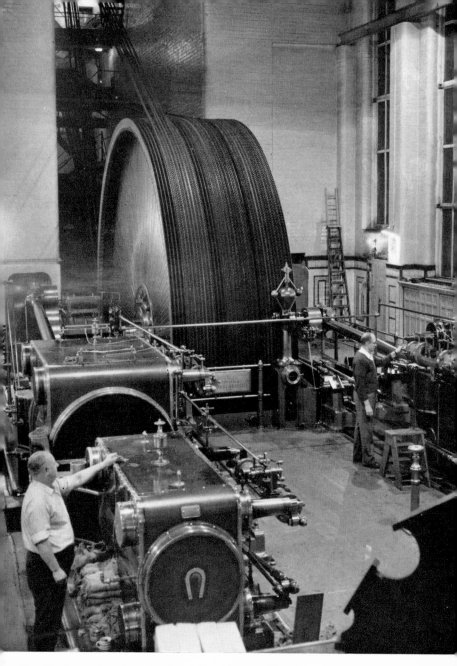

Plate 28. A now obsolete engine house of a spinning mill.

affect the hearing of the operatives. From time to time half-hearted attempts have been made to render looms less noisy, but without any effect on practice, and new fly-shuttle looms are as noisy as old. Noise is accepted by the industry; the operatives have learned to live with it and the older ones, at least, can converse by lip-reading. There are signs, however, that reformers are not satisfied with the situation. The newer types of 'weaving machine' are much quieter.

Weaving sheds vary in appearance. The older ones tend to be crowded with looms, and accessories such as belt drives and dobbies add to the apparent clutter (contrast Plates 32 and 33). Where staple yarns are woven there is a good deal of loose fibre and size-dust shed from the warp yarn floating about. This settles on the looms, which have to be cleaned every few days, and on the members of the structure of the shed to create an untidy appearance. Sheds weaving filament yarns are altogether cleaner. It is difficult to avoid pieces of waste yarn from falling on to the floor, and this has to be swept up twice a shift. The looms and floor in Plate 32 are in a relatively clean state, those in Plate 33 are exceptionally so. Between the two wars warps for some cloths were heavily sized, often with mixings containing china clay, and these would produce much dust and 'fly'.

At one time, say, up to the late 1920s, cotton weaving was thought to require a very damp atmosphere, and it probably did. Consequently most mills were artificially humidified, often by such crude means as injecting steam from jets distributed through the shed, and many were uncomfortably damp. The situation was thought to require control under the Factory Acts, and some not very effective regulations were in force. Gradually, practices have changed; very damp conditions are no longer thought to be necessary and most, if not all, sheds are comfortable in this respect—a relative humidity of about 70 per cent is considered to be high enough. I think that the change has been much helped by improvements in sizing. The weaving of yarns of man-made fibres has always been recognized as

---

Plate 29. Mons spinning mill at Todmorden. The houses behind the mill were mostly built between the wars. The bowling green in the foreground is not private to the mill.

Plate 30. A modern room with ring spinning frames. As is usual in Lancashire, the new frames have been installed in an old mill, often in the place of mules. The pillars are sometimes awkwardly spaced in relation to the dimensions of the frames, but as they are part of the structure that cannot be avoided. The rails in the foreground are for a small trolley that transports rovings and yarns. The trunk of a travelling blower is at some distance to the right of the spinner.

G

requiring relatively dry conditions, and relative humidities of 60–65 per cent are high enough. But for trouble-free weaving of high-quality cloths of all fibres, constancy of atmospheric conditions is important, and an efficient air-conditioning plant is part of the standard equipment of a modern shed.

Apart from the deleterious effects of noise, the chief health hazard for people in the weaving shed is being injured by a flying shuttle. Sometimes something goes wrong and the shuttle, instead of moving along its proper path in the loom, is deflected outwards towards the weaver's alley and, with its speed of forty feet per second and its pointed ends, can cause serious injury. The factory inspectors, employers, and trade unionists are very concerned about this. Guards are fitted to the looms to minimize damage, but so far none has been invented that is completely effective and yet allows the looms to continue working. There are about sixty accidents from flying shuttles a year that involve absence from work of three days or more. 'Weaver's cough' is hardly ever heard of in these days, probably because atmospheric conditions have improved (for example warp sizes sometimes contained zinc chloride in the earlier years, and this could produce an irritant dust). 'Shuttle kissing' was once a necessary, and allegedly harmful, practice. When the weaver had replenished the shuttle with a new cop or bobbin she had to get the thread through the shuttle eye, and this she did by sucking with her mouth. During the 1920s less objectionable ways of threading shuttles were introduced—the factory inspectors urged that any device should make shuttle kissing impossible as well as unnecessary. Shuttle kissing is now a thing of the past.

Over the years the working life of the weaver and the psychological atmosphere of the weaving shed have changed. In the 1920s she would not only do the essential tasks of mending warp and weft breaks and replenishing shuttles with weft, which might occupy one-third of her time, and generally supervising to ensure that the loom was working properly and that good cloth was being produced, for which a further one-third of her time would be available, but she would also have the ancillary tasks of fetching weft from the store, unrolling cloth at the loom and carrying it to the warehouse, and sweeping and cleaning. Her day would develop a pattern. At starting time she would be at her looms waiting for the mill engine to start (lateness was made a very uncomfortable misdemeanour). Slowly the shafting and belting would gather speed, and when it was going fast enough she would start her looms one after the other, so that in the shed the clatter of individual looms working here and there in the shed would quickly build up to a continuous roar. After an hour or two of routine weaving she would go to the store for a can of weft (and possibly a gossip and a cup of tea), her neighbour keeping an eye on her looms the while. Then she might continue routine weaving, perhaps keeping an eye on her neighbour's looms for a time. Towards the end of the spell, a sweeping brush would be passed from weaver to weaver along the weaver's alley (Plate 32), each weaver sweeping her own section of the floor and pushing the accumulating pile of dirt along to the next until at the end of the alley a cleaner would collect it for removal. Then the weaver would don her hat and coat, and continue routine weaving at the looms until the engine began to slow down, at which she would quickly stop the looms and join the rush out of the shed. This would be repeated for the afternoon spell. In winter the passage of time would be additionally marked by lighting-up. Each loom would have a gas-light and all the hundreds of lamps would be controlled from a central point. When the gas was turned on, the overlookers would quickly walk along the alleys with lighted tapers, setting the lamps alight before too much gas had escaped into the atmosphere.

On Friday afternoons the looms would be stopped for two hours or so; all the weavers would set to and clean their looms and the shed cleaners would sweep up and remove the debris so that by the end of the afternoon the whole shed would be shipshape. No weaver would choose to clean looms, but there was an atmosphere of cheerful activity (carolling was indulged in) during this period, and the shed seemed to be a different sort of place with the looms silent.

The regular routine would be broken by other ancillary tasks. Four or so times a week, at irregular intervals, the cloth roller on one or other loom would become full; the weaver would unroll the cloth and roughly plait it (pile it in folds) at the stopped loom, cursorily examining it the while and removing loose threads and minor blemishes. She would interrupt this task every now and then to attend to the other looms in her charge, which would continue weaving, and it might take the best part of an hour to complete. Then, at a convenient time, she would take the cloth to the warehouse. Occasionally a minor disaster would occur with the weaving on one loom—perhaps a bunch of several warp threads would be broken together—and this would overshadow the morning's or afternoon's work. Correction would take an hour or two, the weaver would divide attention between the one stopped loom and the others in her charge, and all the time would have at the back of her mind the uncomfortable thought that the stopped loom was not producing any wage.

All these tasks and happenings had their frustrations and occasional anxieties, but they gave variety and interest to the weaver's work. This interest would be enhanced when, say, once in four to six weeks, the warp on a loom ran out and was replaced by one for a somewhat different cloth. Interest was further enhanced for those who wove fancy cloths. But the traditional weaving set-up was inefficient by modern standards. One by one the ancillary tasks were given to special operatives, and cloth sorts tended to be standardized, so that now in the most efficient modern set-ups the weaver has little to do but monotonously patrol, say, thirty or more looms, mending an occasional warp break, and calling the overlooker's attention when something is apparently going wrong with the looms.

Departments of a weaving mill other than the shed are ordinarily quiet places, not artificially humidified, and heated for the comfort of the people working there. Cloth examination is usually done at one end of the cloth warehouse, and there is a good north-facing window so that defects can easily be seen. It is here that the weaver has pointed out to her (sometimes in unkind terms) serious defects that she has allowed to appear in the cloth she has woven. Until recent times fines would be deducted from her wages for defects.

The production of a weaving mill is not closely integrated as is that of the card room of a spinning mill. The natural unit of production is a set of warper's beams containing enough yarn to produce, say, twenty weaver's beams, each 1,000 to 2,000 yards long. This set may be supplied by the spinner or (for continuous filament yarns) the fibre producer, and will be sized in one go during one or two days. The warps of one set must have the same particulars but each set can be different. The length of the set determines the minimum economical length of any one order of warps that can be processed. The twenty weaver's beams are drawn-in and made ready for the loom in a few days, and then are put into the looms, distributed over the shed, as they become empty. In the meantime, weft has been ordered and is supplied to the weavers from the weft store as required. A warp takes several weeks to weave out. Woven cloth is taken from the loom in pieces each of about 100 yards, inspected in the warehouse, and bundled and stored until deliveries are called for. Mostly, cloth is made to specific order to be delivered as the merchant instructs, but delay in giving instructions sometimes involves months of storage at the manufacturer's—and delay in receiving payment, especially when trade is bad.

It is a function of production control to organize the supply and progress of warps and weft so as to keep the looms busy and meet delivery dates.

One weaving shed can economically produce a wide variety of cloths—a variety that can be increased by having different weaves and wefts with warps of the same particulars. But experience in producing particular cloths is a factor and long runs are very helpful for achieving efficiency. Generally, mass production of a limited range of cloths tends to be in sheds with automatic looms, and production of a wide variety of cloths in sheds with Lancashire looms. Often the latter sheds are zoned so that, for example, jacquard and plain looms are in alternate rows and a weaver will attend to some of each. A good deal of fancy cloth is produced. This involves hand work and does not easily lend itself to mass production. It is a field where the small unit can find scope.

FINISHING WORKS

A finishing works (not mill) consists of a collection of single-storied buildings, sometimes somewhat rambling owing to piecemeal enlargements, with two-storied blocks for offices and warehouses (Plate 34). It is situated where there is water in plenty, usually in a Pennine valley, and a storage reservoir is an important feature.

There is a 'grey room' where customers' unfinished cloth is stored while awaiting processing. The processing rooms are in the single-storied parts. Where liquids are used in open vats the floor is apt to be wet from spilt liquid, and in addition the bleach croft is festooned with 'ropes' of cloth passing from one part of the process to the next (as in Plate 21). When it is realized that twenty to thirty gallons of water are used in finishing a pound of cloth, a general impression of wetness in parts of the works is not surprising, and clogs continue to provide the best form of footwear. In the dyeing department there are open vessels of hot liquor which produce an atmosphere the steaminess of which depends on the effectiveness of the ventilating extractors. Some areas, notably where stenters and baking chambers are situated, are hot and dry. Completely continuous processing is rare, so that a striking feature of a works is the many trucks of partly processed, and often wet, cloth in transit from one process to another. Plan and order there must be, but it is not apparent in the confusion. Finished cloth is inspected and folded and batched to the customer's requirements in the 'making-up' room. Cloth leaves this room in the form in which it is sent to the garment-maker or appears on the shelves of the piece-goods shop.

Different batches of cloth require different combinations of processing, and there is full scope for the arts of the production planner in ensuring that the processes are operated economically, without unduly short runs, and all the cloth receives its appropriate treatments without undue delay. The interval between a batch of cloth entering and leaving the finishing works is several weeks long, depending on the pressure of work on the finisher and the processes involved.

One problem of finishing works that in recent years has become increasingly difficult and expensive to solve is the disposal of effluents. Many decades ago the Irwell, Mersey, and some other rivers and streams were ruined by works pouring effluents into them without restraint. Now the River Boards and Local Authorities are placing ever more exacting restrictions on the condition of effluents they will receive, and elaborate methods of treatment have to be adopted by the works.

Every spinning, doubling, and weaving mill worthy of the name has a laboratory for testing and examining fibres, yarns, and cloths (Plate 35), and every finishing works a chemical laboratory. Spinning and weaving mills do not normally have research departments and only the large finishing works do. The industry relies heavily on the Research Association for these services, but the large combines are tending to establish research facilities of their own.

The Lancashire mill or works has, in addition to technical departments, the ancillary departments of any factory—the office, the canteen (Plate 36), the first-aid room (Plate 37). Mention has already been made (p. 13) of the nurseries for the children of mothers working in the mill, established in the early post-war years when labour was short.

Lancashire mills and works are more than places where goods are produced, profits (or losses) are made, and opportunities for investment are provided. They present a way of life as well as a livelihood for the workers. In this they are not, of course, different from other factories. To write fully about this requires more intimate knowledge of mill life than I possess, but even from occasional and superficial contacts I have obtained some impressions.

Most of the operatives live near 't'mill', and for these it is part of their lives. Many go home to dinner, and home and workplace are closely associated. Sometimes families have been closely associated with particular mills for two or more generations, and many of the older workers, if their mill closes, leave the industry rather than transfer to another mill. Married women ex-operatives may be known to the manager who will send for them at short notice and ask them to substitute for someone who is away ill. Some of the older operatives have tended to regard the machines they look after as 'their' machines—an attitude that has to be countered if there is redeployment. Social activities are organized, and common customs such as decorating the mill at Christmastime and subscribing to wedding presents and funeral wreaths are observed. According to one custom, any likely male from the office who was foolhardy enough to walk through the shed at Christmastime was heartily kissed by the girl weavers. He was then expected to contribute towards the cost of the Christmas 'footings'—a feast of meat-pies, cakes, and drinks taken into the mill just before the close-down for the holiday. Possibly more organized canteen parties have killed this custom. Some mills have sports teams. All these are probably as much expressions as causes of a corporate spirit, and they are not often so strong as to cause mill workers to withdraw from the social life of the locality in which they live.

There are, or at least were, social conventions in the mill. Thus in a weaving mill winding is more highly regarded than weaving even though it is not as highly paid. Roving frame tenters have regarded themselves as better than slubber tenters. Loom overlookers have been regarded as a race apart in a weaving mill, and the attitude finds expression in 'tacklers' tales' which typically display some act of stupidity. In the weaving shed cloth lookers were traditionally disliked. Some of them seemed almost to enjoy the task of chiding weavers who produced defective cloth.

In the 1920s clogs and shawls were still commonly worn. Clogs are very comfortable, especially on the hard and sometimes damp floors of weaving sheds and finishing works, and the clogger's shop was an essential part of the urban scene. Weaving and other under-managers used to wear, as a kind of uniform, a close-fitting black cap.

I have been told by an ex-spinner that even up to the early 1930s the progress of a mule spinner in Bolton would be marked by the following stages. First he would come from school as a little piecer; he would wear a scarf and cap, and would carry his dinner in a basin wrapped in a red handkerchief. On promotion to cross piecer he would receive 1s. a week increase in wages and change from a red to a white handkerchief for his dinner. On promotion to side piecer he would receive 10s. a week increase in wages and it would be accept-able for him to wear a collar and tie when going to and from work and carry his dinner in a container other than a basin. As a spinner he would have still more freedom of dress. As an overlooker, the highest stage, he would necessarily wear a collar and tie and carry his dinner in a small Gladstone bag. He would wear a trilby hat if formerly he had been a spinner, or a bowler hat if he had formerly been a fitter (an alternative route of promotion). At some time, I was not told when, there would be a change from clogs to shoes. At one time—at least until 1916—the newcomer to mule spinning in Oldham suffered an initiation ceremony of having his private parts daubed with black oil.

A notable feature of mule spinning was the payment of a piece rate to the spinner, or 'minder', who would then pay his piecers a fixed wage. The minder received a fixed allowance for consumable stores, which he used at his own discretion to maintain the condition of the mules. He regarded the mules as his own, and some minders who 'accepted' mules on installation in 1905 were still operating the same pair when man and machines were superannuated three or four decades later.

The customs and social activities of any society induce and express a sense of belonging that gives satisfaction to the participants and encourages loyalty to the society. But they are the products of stability and are inimical to change. Lancashire mills and works have provided such stability, at least until the last decade or so. How much of mill life, as it has been known, can survive current changes, and whether a new stability can be established, remain to be seen. But the outlook is not promising. Widespread mill closures and the rapid adoption of labour-saving machines and practices, with ac-

companying redundancies, must destroy the sense of security
operatives have had in their jobs; and the spread of night-shift
working makes mill life less attractive than it was. These help to
increase the material standard of living and, in textiles at least, seem
to be essential for industrial survival. But for the workers the effect
must be to make working life an experience apart from ordinary
life instead of a part of it.

FIRMS AND THE INDUSTRY

Basically the industry is organized in four main 'horizontal' sections:
spinning, weaving (termed manufacturing), finishing, and merchanting. There are also small sections such as doubling, and condenser
spinning and manufacturing, and for some purposes the finishing
section is subdivided into bleaching, dyeing, calico printing, and so
on. Traditionally most firms belonged to one section and, although
amalgamations have altered the picture for ownership, the traditional
horizontal structure still influences the way in which the industry
goes about its business.

The spinning firm produces yarns to the order of cloth or hosiery
manufacturers or other customers although, making a product that
has many outlets, it will often also make for stock. It finances its
operations until the yarn is sold. The manufacturer makes to the
order of the merchant converter, financing the operation and
receiving payment after the cloth has been delivered to the merchant
converter's instructions. Delay in receiving such instructions sometimes causes distress, especially when trade is bad. The manufacturer will sometimes make standard goods for stock. The finisher
works on commission, processing cloth that is the property of his
customers—mostly merchants—and charging for his services. The
merchant converter decides in detail what cloth shall be made and
sold, gives instructions to the manufacturer and finisher, and is
financially responsible from the time the grey cloth leaves the manufacturer until the finished cloth is sold.

In the heyday of the industry, most firms belonged to one or other
section, but with the passage of time many variations in organization have developed, and many firms now cover more than one
section. From early times there have been firms with both spinning
and weaving, the processes often being closely integrated to produce
a few standard lines of goods. In recent years such integrated units

have constituted roughly one-tenth of the industry. (This ratio i
computed from the number of spindles in firms belonging to th
United Kingdom Textile Manufacturers' Association as a fractio
of the total number in the industry.) In the early years after Worl
War II some merchants bought weaving concerns to ensure thei
supplies of cloth; more recently weaving concerns have bough
merchanting houses to ensure an off-take for their products. Severa
firms brand their products. One large firm has spinning and weavin
mills and retail shops. The 'big four' combines have absorbed firm
from all sections of the industry, and a few smaller independent firm
also cover a wide range.

Common ownership does not necessarily imply technical an
managerial integration of the constituent mills, works, and businesses
The extent of such integration can be known only to people in th
firms. It varies from almost no integration to close integration fo
the complete manufacture and marketing of a limited range of goods
and within each firm the situation is doubtless developing—fast i
the recently formed combines. However close the integration, th
four sections tend to be run as departments or divisions, each with
degree of autonomy. Seldom is a vertically integrated firm entirel
self-contained. A spinning mill cannot economically spin as wide
range of yarns as a weaving mill can profitably use, and since ther
is a good market for yarn (e.g. to hosiery and carpet manufacturer
and for export as well as to weavers), the spinning mill in a combin
will sell to outside firms, and the weaving mill will buy from outsid
spinners. Likewise it is not economical to link closely the production
of a finishing works with that of one or two weaving mills. All thes
factors make the interpretation of statistics of the ownership of mill
difficult. And because of them the horizontal division of the industr
has persisted.

A detailed account of the sizes of mills and firms, and of develop
ments in these up to the early post-war years is given by Dr. R
Robson; here is given a brief description only. The typical spinnin
mill employs one or two hundred operatives. Mills vary in siz
according to their age and the tex (coarseness) of the yarn spu
(newer mills and those spinning finer yarns tend to be larger)
80 per cent being in 1948 contained within a range of four to one i
size. There are still firms with one or two mills, and at the other en
of the scale are the former Fine Spinners' and Doublers' Associatio
(formed in 1898) and the Lancashire Cotton Corporation, now a par

of Courtaulds and run as a single division comprising about one-quarter of the spinning industry.

Weaving sheds are more variable in size, 80 per cent in 1948 being contained within a range of about twenty to one; a few mammoth mills had about 2,000 looms compared with fewer than 100 in the smallest. Many mills had 400–500 looms and employed 100–200 operatives. Up to the early post-war years the 'room and power' system was in vogue, according to which a small firm would rent a portion of a large weaving shed together with heating, lighting, and mechanical power and would install and run as few as fifty looms, the owner doing much of the work himself and employing a dozen or so operatives. The production of specialized products requires more and closer managerial and technical supervision than that of long runs of standard lines, and so the former has tended to be concentrated in the smaller mills. The modern tendency is for mills, even those producing standard lines, to have fewer looms than before, automatic and run for two or three shifts a day. There has been some grouping of weaving mills in horizontal combines, but most grouping seems to have been in combines covering a range of processes.

The individual finishing works with a few exceptions in 1954 employed anything from 50 to 400 operatives. Besides individual concerns there have been large combines since the beginning of the century.

Firms of merchant converters in 1954 varied enormously in size, from 158 each dealing with fewer than 10,000 square yards of cloth a year to forty-three each dealing with over ten million square yards. The fragmentation of the market among so many of them (nearly 2,000 in 1954) has been much criticized. In reply it is pointed out that most of the trade is handled by the big firms: 60 per cent of the yardage was in 1954 handled by the biggest 6 per cent of firms; over 70 per cent by the biggest 16 per cent of firms; and so on. The enormous reduction in trade since 1954 and the spectacular amalgamations that have taken place have doubtless altered the picture considerably.

In discussions on the problems of Lancashire over the past forty or more years vertical integration has from time to time been advocated as a panacea—the discussion has been at its most vague when the change has been termed rationalization. By the test of experience it is hard to see that it, or any other form of organization, provides the key to success in textile operation. In Lancashire almost every conceivable form of organization into firms has existed; from individual mills each covering one process and specializing in a narrow range of products to large horizontal combines producing a wide range, or to vertical combines embracing spinning and weaving, spinning and weaving and finishing, weaving and merchanting, spinning and weaving and merchanting, and so on. Within the vertical combines the degree of integration of processes has varied from almost none to the closest that is feasible, and the range of products has varied from a narrow one to a wide one. If any of these forms had been generally and markedly superior, surely that fact would have emerged and the superior form would have survived as the predominating form. In fact, this has not happened, and the variety of form is almost as great as it ever was, the main change being in the size of the firm.

Vertical integration is held to have commercial advantages in reducing the number of points of transfer between firms, at each of which a profit is extracted. But integration does not reduce the capital employed and it is hard to see how it can reduce the necessary profit margin in total. There would be an advantage if integration reduced management and administrative costs, but the scope for such saving is not likely to be large since the integrated firm needs internal controls. The chief advantage I can think of would come from a reduction in sales staff. One economic advantage can come if, say, the spinning mill is not large enough to keep the weaving mill supplied. Then fluctuations in demand for yarn and cloth can be met by varying the amount of yarn bought outside and keeping the firm's spinning mill fully occupied at all times, or more fully occupied than would be otherwise possible. This kind of thing can be done only if there is a substantial horizontal spinning section of the industry to supply yarn (and carry the main burden of fluctuations in demand).

Another advantage can come from integrating weaving with merchanting, or even with supply to the consumer. Under a horizontal organization year-by-year fluctuations in consumer demand cause fluctuations in the stocks of cloth at various points in such a way as to make the fluctuations in orders to weavers greater than those in consumer demand. Integration should make it possible to reduce or eliminate this effect.

The technical advantages of vertical integration can be considerable. There is great variety in the fibres, yarns, finishes, and processes that can be used to produce a cloth for a given end-use, and the processes interact so that what is done at one stage affects what should be done at another. The economical and efficient production of the final cloth requires a close integration of all these. This may be easier to achieve in a single firm than in separate ones, and an enterprising manager may feel that he can do better with all processes under his control than by having to deal with autonomous managers of other mills. Further, if production and sales are closely and permanently linked, the mass-production of standard lines can be organized with confidence to the extent that the market permits; and it is possible that the development of profitable new lines is facilitated. But difficulties of communication and control within firms are not unknown, and many horizontal firms have effectively developed forms of mutual co-operation that secure many of the technical advantages of combination into a single firm. The quality and spirit of the managers involved are possibly more important than the form of commercial organization.

Full vertical integration has its difficulties and disadvantages, as well as its advantages. It requires exceptionally high quality of management to co-ordinate all the activities, secure communication of information between departments and disciplined action, and at the same time provide scope for the exercise of enterprise and enthusiasm by people along the line. A unit that is set up to secure all the advantages of integration is apt to be inflexible, and not to be readily responsive to the changes in fashion and demand that are characteristic of much of the textile trade. It is likely that small and medium-sized independent mills, horizontally organized, will continue to serve sections of the market efficiently, and to contribute to the prosperity of the industry. However, the whole question is being closely examined in the Textile Council's 1967–8 productivity study (see p. 117), and more authoritative conclusions than are so far available are to be hoped for.

There are in Lancashire many firms that, although not part of the industry, are very closely associated with it. Prominent among these are the textile machinery makers. Lancashire mills now import much machinery from abroad, and the Lancashire machinists export most of their products. Nevertheless the natural connection between the machinists and the industry on the doorstep remains very strong. New developments in machines are first tried out in local mills, and the technologists contribute notably to the spread of technical knowledge in Lancashire. In addition to the large firms that make spinning machinery, winding machinery, looms, and finishing machinery there are a host of small firms producing largely consumable ancillary equipment. These include makers of bobbins and paper tubes, spinning rings and travellers, coverings for spinning rollers, card wire, healds and reeds, shuttles, and pickers. Suppliers of starches, chemicals, dyestuffs, and oils have wider connections but their Lancashire connections are important.

WAGE SYSTEMS

In many jobs in the industry output depends a good deal on the skill and effort of the individual operative, and that of each operative can be readily measured by weighing yarn or measuring cloth, or by reading an indicator on a machine. For these payment is by piece rates which until World War II were prescribed by lists applying to districts or to the whole industry. In spinning the unions and employers' associations were strong enough to prevent individual mills from negotiating their own rates, and when in the 1930s the pressures of bad trade and unemployment depressed weavers' wages in some mills below the levels prescribed by the list, the list was made legally enforceable. These lists, which had been developed over many decades, allowed for a multitude of variations in processing conditions and product particulars, and purported to ensure that whatever the conditions and particulars each operative would receive each week a wage appropriate to the skill and effort applied.

The Uniform List, which determined the wages of most weavers on non-automatic looms, was adopted by the whole industry towards the end of the nineteenth century. In effect it prescribed the fraction of a penny to be paid for each pick (weft thread) woven, and from this and the cloth particulars it was a matter of simple arithmetic to calculate the price to be paid for weaving a piece of cloth of given length. There was a basic price per pick for standard conditions and particulars, and this was adjusted by percentage additions and subtractions, made in a certain order, to allow for deviations from the standard in such particulars as the fineness of the yarns, the closeness of the setting of the warp threads, the cloth width, the length of yarn on the weft package, the complication of the weave, the number of colours in the weft, and the number of warp beams involved; and there was, later, an addition if the yarn was of 'artificial silk' (man made fibre). Account was also taken of such conditions as weaving a arrow cloth in a wide loom. Some of the adjustments were finely graded, some were little more than a crude recognition that some factor was relevant; in total they were substantial and they made the calculation of the rate to be paid per pick a complicated business. They had been negotiated between employers and unions over many years, but the principles that guided the negotiations and decisions re unknown. It seems, however, that in a vague way account was taken of the amount of work involved (without the guidance given by work study), the skill required to weave the finer and more complicated cloths, the responsibility involved in supervising valuable machinery and textile materials, and the profitability of the more costly cloths. From time to time new complications were added to the list to accommodate new technical developments, e.g. the introduction of 'artificial silk' in the 1920s and the increase in looms per weaver above the traditional four in the 1930s. Agreement on these was reached only after long negotiation, sometimes accompanied by strife.

In the early years of this century this system was doubtless (and with justification) regarded as being advanced and enlightened, and the industry was satisfied with it. It provided justice, albeit rough, between weavers, it provided manufacturers with a fair competitive basis, and (while it was observed) it protected weavers from lowered wages through under-cutting. It did not apply to automatic looms but they were too few to attract attention. However, the adjustments that were made in the 1930s to allow for more looms per weaver were made only with great difficulty, and many people began to feel that the system was too rigid and unrealistic to be applicable in the times of rapid technical change that were coming. The employers' associations studied the problem and had worked out tentative proposals for reform by the time the war came.

In 1948 the Government appointed the Cotton Manufacturing Commission, consisting of representatives of the employers and the operatives and of independent people from outside the industry, to examine the whole question and make proposals. The Commission decided that weavers should in principle be paid for the quantity of work done, as measured by work study (variations in quality of work, i.e. in the relative skills required for different operations, were regarded as too insignificant to justify complications their recognition would produce), so that any reduction in the work content of a piece of cloth achieved by technical improvements, or in any other way, would be accompanied by a reduction in the wage cost

per piece, although the weaver's wages would be safeguarded. It also
found that in non-automatic weaving about one-third of the weaver'
time should be allowed for patrolling and general supervision, and
that of the measurable work about two-thirds, on average, wa
devoted to the two elements of replenishing weft and mending war
breaks. The Commission therefore proposed a new list based on thes
two elements, which could be estimated by direct observation or b
calculation for any given cloth and set of looms—a system based no
on full work study at the individual mill, but on an approximatio
to a work study assessment. According to this principle, the numbe
of looms in the charge of the weaver, which was a prominent featur
of the Uniform List, was irrelevant. The Commission was unable t
adhere rigidly to its principle but, for political reasons rather tha
from conviction, allowed for slightly higher wages to be earned a
the number of looms in the weaver's complement increased abov
the traditional four. Later an addition (which had its roots in trad
ition) was also made for the weaving of man-made fibres.

The C.M.C. system, as it was called, was adopted as an optiona
alternative to the Uniform List, and its use has extended, although i
is reported[1] that even in 1966 the Uniform List continued in use in
few firms. The list for weavers of non-automatic looms was th
Commission's *tour de force*. Assessment of wages for automati
weaving was left largely to work study in individual mills, which ha
been made possible and acceptable by the spread of understanding o
the subject among managers and trade union officials and by th
training of staff to carry it out. Only brief attention was paid to th
wage payment to other operatives in the manufacturing section of th
industry.

A parallel Commission for the spinning section reported in 1945
At that time there were six district lists in use, 90 per cent of th
industry being covered by the Bolton and Oldham lists. The Com
mission did not envisage the adoption of any fundamentally nev

[1] By G. B. Fielding in the centenary brochure of the United Kingdom Textil
Manufacturers' Association.

Plate 31. A weaving shed in the Rossendale Valley, near Haslingden. Note th
mixture of factories, houses, hen runs, fields, railway, and ways (rather tha
roads).

Plate 32. An old-fashioned weaving shed with non-automatic looms closel
packed and driven by belts from overhead shafting. The passageway is th
weaver's alley, where weavers do most of their work.

rinciples but recommended a tidying up of the situation by the doption of 'universal' lists. It proposed one for mule spinning, which vas adopted as the Evershed List (named after the chairman of the Commission), and for ring spinning and its associated occupations ts recommendations were made the basis of negotiations which esulted in the Aronson List (named after the chairman of the egotiating body). These had the kinds of weakness and strength lready described for the weaving Uniform List. They tended to lay own stereotyped rules for the staffing of machines, and they took nadequate account of the elements of the operatives' work load— otably the frequency of yarn and roving breaks in processing which vas only recognized in the proviso that this should not be excessive. 3ut they gave rough justice between operatives and stability. However, the decline of mule spinning has deflected attention away from he corresponding problems of wage payment, and the revolutionary hanges that have occurred in ring spinning and other related pro- esses have caused the employers' association and unions to concen- rate on securing an acceptance of the use of work study for making rrangements at individual mills. These efforts reached success in the Manchester Agreement of 1964, according to which the central odies approve the individual mill schemes, chiefly in ensuring that he resulting weekly wages come within certain centrally agreed bands.

Plate 33. A modern weaving shed, built during 1966, with automatic looms weaving cloths for linings, rainwear, and anoraks, from filament yarns of man- made fibre. The building embodies the most advanced principles of weaving-shed construction—free from pillars, windowless, fully insulated against heat loss, and air-conditioned. It works for 120 hours a week.

Plate 34. A finishing works in the hills near to Bolton. The chimney is undergoing repair.

H

CHAPTER 5

Workers' and Employers' Organizations

The many organizations and institutions that serve the Lancashire textile industry have had a long history, some of them deriving from movements early in the nineteenth century. They were mostly developed, in their number and complexity, to serve the enormous industry as it was before World War I. Between the two wars, despite contraction in the size of the industry, the institutions changed but little—the chief changes added to their number. In the second half of the 1950s people began to feel that there were too many organizations, and the 1960s are seeing a reduction in their number through amalgamation.

This chapter describes the trade unions, the trade associations, and the Textile Council. Other organizations are described in Chapter 6.

TRADE UNIONS [1]

Extreme decentralization and rich variety are the marks of Lancashire textile trade unions. In each sizeable town or district there is an autonomous union for each main occupation or small group of occupations in the mill. The district unions for each craft are joined in the amalgamations listed in the table opposite. All these amalgamations are based on Lancashire and their activities are largely confined to that county and surrounding areas. They are usually thought of as the Lancashire textile trade unions, sometimes yet as the cotton unions, and are the subject of this section.

There are also other unions operating in the textile industry of the county, which will merely be mentioned in passing. The National Union of Dyers, Bleachers and Textile Workers, based on Bradford, and the Guild of Calico Printers', Bleachers', Dyers' and Finishers' Foremen, based on Lancashire but having jurisdiction as far afield as Carlisle, serve operatives in the finishing section of the industry. A

[1] For full information see H. A. Turner, *Trade Union Growth, Structure and Policy: A Comparative Study of the Cotton Unions*, Allen & Unwin, London, 1962.

List of Trade Unions serving the
Lancashire Textile Industry

Spinning Section
Amalgamated Association of Operative Spinners and Twiners
National Association of Card, Blowing and Ring Room Operatives
(since September 1968 renamed the National Union of Textile and
  Allied Workers)

Weaving Section
Amalgamated Association of Beamers, Twisters and Drawers
Amalgamated Weavers' Association
General Union of Associations of Loom Overlookers
Lancashire Amalgamated Tape Sizers' Association
Amalgamated Tape Sizers' Friendly Protection Society
Amalgamated Textile Warehousemen
General Union of Lancashire and Yorkshire Warpdressers' Associations

---

few textile operatives such as some doublers belong to the National
Union of General and Municipal Workers, and workers in mills who
do jobs common to many industries, such as electricians, engineers,
and transport drivers, belong to appropriate national unions.

Among the unions listed there is variation in size, ranging (in
1967) from 34,451 in the weavers' amalgamation and 24,203 in
the cardroom amalgamation to 1,860 in the beamers', etc., amalgamation. The spinners' amalgamation, which covers only mule spinners
and was once among the big unions, was in 1967 down to 1,192 and
is still declining.

The unions vary in the number of occupations covered. The
cardroom amalgamation is almost a general union, covering almost
all operatives in a ring spinning mill: blowroom men, card strippers
and grinders (the aristocrats of the union who dominate its affairs),
card tenters, drawframe tenters, speedframe tenters, ring spinners,
and doffers are the main groups. The weavers' amalgamation,
although made up largely of weavers, caters also for a few winders
and beamers. The overlookers' union and tape sizers' association, on
the other hand, are exclusive to those particular occupations—they
are narrowly based craft unions as ordinarily understood.

There is variation in the degree of 'openness', as Professor H. A.

Turner puts it.[1] Any worker who can get a job in a ring spinning mill or as a weaver can join the appropriate union—these are 'open' unions. Entry to the 'closed' tape sizers' and overlookers' unions, on the other hand, is very vigilantly controlled—it is a great help to a candidate to have a father or uncle who is a member. The closed unions are able virtually to prevent the employment of non-unionist in their occupations, so that these unions regulate entry to their occupations. The open unions have not so far been able to enforce the 'closed shop', although the employers' associations have gone so far as to say that they prefer the operatives to be union members. I have been told that approximately 60 per cent of weavers are union members; a secretary of a cardroom union has claimed 80–90 per cent membership.

There is variety in the extent to which the district unions are controlled by their respective amalgamations but, although membership of an amalgamation must mean some loss of independence, the basic autonomy remains and is jealously guarded. Each district union has its own funds, parts of them being for unemployment and funeral benefits, and each adopts its own policy in the caution or profligacy with which these funds are used. One impediment to the joining of two districts is sometimes the fact that one union is much richer than the other. The amalgamation works out the general union policy towards wages, working conditions, hours of work, attitude to multi-shift working, changes in labour arrangements, and so on. But there is room for variation in the interpretation and application of such policy, and variation between districts occurs, to such a degree that the amalgamation policy can be almost flouted. For example, spinning employers during the early post-war years found the Bolton cardroom union most helpful and encouraging in making changes for improving efficiency in their mills; spinners in the Rochdale and Oldham areas complained that their union officials drove protection of the interests of the workers to the point of making the necessary changes difficult to achieve. (These oppositions are past.) The district union sometimes enters into agreements with the local employers' association to govern some condition of work for all the mills in the district.

The key man in the district union is the secretary, a full-time official in a larger and part-time in a smaller union. Although coming under the jurisdiction of an elected committee he can (and often does)

---

[1] Op. cit., p. 139.

have a strong influence on the way the union's affairs are run and hence on the way the mills operate in the district. This he achieves through his ability and strength of character and his close knowledge of the mills and people of the district; and the result is inevitably affected by his temperament and prejudices. Of course, he would not be elected to the position if he were not the sort of man the committee liked, and he would not retain it if he could not carry the committee with him. As time goes on, however, trust and strong loyalties may develop to strengthen his influence. The district union secretary often takes a prominent part in the life of his locality, usually as town councillor or justice of the peace. And almost invariably he is a member of the Labour Party. 'Commies' and near-communists are not unknown among trade union officers, but they are regarded as oddities rather than a serious factor.

Most of the district secretary's time is taken up in dealing with individual operatives and managers. If the operative has some grievance at work, or some difficulty over sick pay or unemployment pay or almost any social matter, he or she can take it to the secretary, who in many towns keeps an office open several evenings in the week. If there is difficulty at a mill involving one operative or a group, the secretary will quickly make contact with the management and attempt to reach a settlement. Sometimes a special payment or some change will be negotiated; sometimes the secretary may tell the operatives that they are being silly, or that the things complained of cannot be altered. In these activities the secretaries help to keep the mills going. There is a procedure for taking mill disputes that cannot be settled to negotiation between the district union and the local employers' association, or even further to the corresponding county bodies. This procedure is slow and is not often used.

Common complaints are that spinning or weaving is bad because of some deterioration in yarn quality which causes too many yarn breaks during processing—too many 'ends down'. Another complaint is that the wage of a particular operative is not correctly calculated. Wage lists in the industry are (as has been noted) very complicated and it is beyond the wit of many operatives to make the necessary calculations; the district secretary (or his assistant) has to be expert in this.

Since the war there have been many changes in mills due to the re-allocation of duties to achieve greater productivity, the installation of new types of equipment, and the adoption of multi-shift working.

Within general agreements that have been made to cover the wages and working conditions associated with these changes, the district secretary has to negotiate the detailed arrangements for each mill and secure the agreement of the operatives directly concerned, who have the last word. In this activity a 'tough' secretary can make change very difficult, an understanding secretary sympathetic to change can help it considerably while protecting the interests of the operatives. Sometimes the union secretary makes up for deficiencies in the management by advising on how to make the proposed new set-up work better. The ease and success with which changes can be made varies not only from district to district but also from mill to mill within a district according to the competence of the management and the confidence the secretary has in its reliability.

With direct contact between the operatives and the district secretary, there is no place for the shop steward common in other industries. Some unions have mill collectors to collect union subscriptions and although these have no constitutional authority and, apparently, little influence, they presumably form an additional channel of communication between the secretary and the rank and file.

The broad policy changes and wage negotiations which are the business of the amalgamations do not involve as much activity as does the day-to-day work of the district unions, and so the amalgamation is run by a very small staff, typically by a full-time secretary with perhaps an assistant in the larger amalgamations and a typist or two. The executive committee is mostly composed of secretaries of the district unions, one of whom is usually the president. Although they have no outstanding authority in their unions, the secretaries of the larger unions are important men in the trade union world and are in some degree county and national public figures. Until recently two of these had seats on the General Council of the Trades Union Congress (now all textile unions share one seat), and in the present-day set-up of the country such a position carries opportunities and responsibilities for public service of which the leaders of the Lancashire unions have taken a share. Public recognition in the form of knighthoods and directorships of the Bank of England has occasionally been accorded, and in January 1968 the Secretary of the Amalgamated Weavers' Association, also Chairman of the T.U.C., became Lord Wright.

With so many unions, inter-union disputes would be expected, but little is heard of such. Inter-union rivalries and competition exist, but over the years conventions have been developed to govern borderline situations and the unions have learnt to live together. Modern developments in production techniques have not aggravated problems of this kind appreciably since they have not involved labour changes that cut across union boundaries.

The habit of living, and positively working, together has found expression in two large combinations covering nearly all the Lancashire textile unions. One is the Northern Counties Textile Trades Federation which includes the amalgamations covering the manufacturing section of the industry. Naturally, all the operatives working in a weaving mill have the same hours of work and this Federation's main object is to further a common policy on such matters. (Presumably, since at the most only two unions are substantially involved in a spinning mill, less formal arrangements suffice to secure consistent policies on hours of work for that section of the industry.)

All the amalgamations except that of the tape-sizers are joined in the United Textile Factory Workers' Association (U.T.F.W.A.). The exact relationships between the amalgamations and the two central bodies are complicated and, to the outsider, obscure; but the U.T.F.W.A. may be regarded as representing the Lancashire textile trade unions as a whole on industrial and political questions. Its effective members are officers of the amalgamations and their constituent unions, and its president and secretary are secretaries of two district unions. It enters into county-wide agreements with the employers' organizations on hours of work and multi-shift working —agreements which are probably best expressed as statements of attitude and general intention rather than as specifying precise action to which any of the parties can be bound. It is the channel through which the unions mainly affiliate with the Labour Party. The U.T.F.W.A. is the agency through which the unions have added their weight to the pressures on the government to reduce imports of cloth from low-cost countries. In 1957 it published a *Plan for Cotton*, proposals worked out by the present Prime Minister for reorganizing the industry. This was abandoned in August 1967 as being unsuitable for the present day.

Generally, Lancashire trade union leaders are regarded as being moderate and progressive and (as the words are understood by employers) 'responsible' and 'statesmanlike'. They are realists in bargaining for wages in a declining industry, and any apparently extravagant claims that may be made for increases are part of the bargaining ritual. Union leaders give weight to the long-term interests of their members, which are bound up in increasing efficiency of production, as well as to today's and tomorrow's wages. Relationships between the employers and unions are good; generally the officials like and respect each other, and many of them are on christian-name terms. The existence of a common enemy in foreign imports strengthens the habit of co-operation.

But the harmony is not without astringency. Anyone working in the industry is conscious that there are two sides that are often in opposition, and the union leaders represent one of those sides vigorously and tenaciously, and sometimes vehemently.

There have been criticisms of the policies and set-up of the Lancashire unions. Professor Turner[1] has suggested that since the war the unions have not pressed hard enough for higher wages, as those in the engineering industries have done, and so have weakened the pressures on managements to install new labour-saving machinery. Such changes as have occurred, and the preference for work-sharing through short-time working, are said to have tended to keep inefficient mills and obsolete machinery in production. Contrary policies, he suggests, would have accelerated the development of a more compact and more efficient industry and would have been better in the long run for the workers. He also points out that even the large amalgamations and the U.T.F.W.A. have very little in the way of professional and research staff to provide information and guidance on these complex matters—although they do avail themselves of outside help, and union officers are responsive to new ideas.

Professor Turner has criticized the unions as being weak at the top, because of the lack of strong centralized government by the amalgamations and the U.T.F.W.A., and weak at the base through the lack of formal organization in the mills. Suggestions have from time to time been put forward within the union movement, and outside, for stronger centralization. Publicists have questioned whether the complicated union structure, which has changed but little for half a century, is suitable for this modern world, although the critics do not always establish clearly in what way the present

[1] Op. cit., pp. 336 *et seq.*

Plate 35. The testing laboratory of a spinning mill.
Plate 36. A mill canteen.

Plate 37. Treatment in a mill first-aid room.
Plate 38. The floor of the Manchester Royal Exchange in 1877.
Plate 39. The floor of the Manchester Royal Exchange on 20 March 1964.

structure is defective and what changes would make things better.

To agree that improvements in the Lancashire unions are possible and desirable is only to acknowledge that these are human institutions, and doubtless the enormous changes that have occurred in the industry over the past few decades will force changes in the unions. Quietly and slowly changes are occurring through the joining of district unions, particularly when a local secretary retires. But large changes are slow to come. The present system has developed over many decades and its roots go deep. Workers, union officers, and employers are accustomed to the present system and know how to operate it. Many people depend on it for their personal position and livelihood. The system works, and there have been no compelling pressures for reform. Suggestions for and discussions of change seem to be as long-standing as the institutions themselves, but the unions have so far been massively slow to take action, although there is now, in 1968, talk of large-scale amalgamation, including an amalgamation between the two large cardroom and weavers' unions.

However, the present system has some advantages. It has surely been one factor in producing industrial peace for thirty years, so that the serious losses in industrial efficiency and well-being that must accompany the frequent strikes and disputes in some other industries have been avoided. The variety in the operations of the decentralized unions ensures that backwardness in any respect in some districts is balanced by forwardness in others. With the forward areas showing the practicability of new methods and ideas, progress may well have been greater than if uniform, but necessarily compromise, policies were followed everywhere.

EMPLOYERS' ORGANIZATIONS

Although Lancashire industrialists are keenly competitive and have a reputation for being strong individualists, they have enough, and strong enough, common interests to induce them to organize in associations, of which there is, in the view of some people, almost a plethora. Between the two wars, and in the early post-war years, although the industry was contracting, the number of organizations increased slightly. One or two were formed largely to protect

---

Plate 40. A typical landscape in a spinning district.
Plate 41. The power station at Kearsley, between Manchester and Bolton, with the River Irwell.

producers against the effects of reduced prices caused by 'weak' selling. Some were formed to serve what were, at the time, thought to be the separate interests of processers of the then emerging rayon. The moods associated with the considerable contraction of the industry in 1961 occasioned some amalgamations. On the whole, however, the structure of employers' organizations still reflects the structure of an industry largely divided into 'horizontal' sections: spinners, manufacturers, and finishers.

The master spinners are organized in the British Spinners' and Doublers' Association (Cotton and Allied Textile Industries), an amalgamation completed in 1961 of the Federation of Master Cotton Spinners' Associations Ltd., the Yarn Spinners' Association, the Rayon Staple Spinners' and Doublers' Association, and the Yarn Doublers' Association. This amalgamation marked the end of the separation of rayon from cotton and of the activities of the Yarn Spinners' Association, proscribed in 1959 by the Restrictive Trade Practices Court, in maintaining yarn prices. The inclusion of the smaller Yarn Doublers' Association was a sensible economy measure.

Manufacturers are organized in the United Kingdom Textile Manufacturers' Association (Cotton, Man-made and Allied Fibres), which was formed in 1961 by amalgamating the Cotton Spinners' and Manufacturers' Association and the Rayon Weavers' Association. This association includes 'vertical' firms that spin and weave.

These two associations are, in a complex way which we need not explore, related to constituent district associations. The district associations deal with local questions, and the central associations with matters affecting the industry as a whole, or with disputes with labour that cannot be resolved locally. In effect, the district employers' associations are the counterparts of the district unions.

These two associations represent the spinning, doubling, and weaving sections of the industry in all matters. They negotiate county agreements with the unions on wages and hours and conditions of work. They look after the interests of their sections of the industry before governments, presenting views and information on such things as tariff and tax changes which are thought to be prejudicial. They safeguard the interests of the employers when regulations are made under the Factory Acts. They negotiate for the industry freight charges, take an interest in electricity charges, and assist firms in presenting cases connected with rating. The spinners' association takes an active interest in anything that happens in the growing countries and the markets to affect the supply of raw cotton, in both quality and quantity. They represent their sections of the industry on such bodies as the Confederation of British Industries, the International Federation of Cotton and Allied Textile Industries, the Liverpool Cotton Association, and the research associations.

In addition to making an impact on the outside world, the associations guide the impact of the outside world on its members. They give information on legislative and fiscal changes that might affect members (e.g. changes in factory regulations) and advise members on how to meet them. The Cotton Industry Act of 1959, with its compensation for firms scrapping redundant machinery and its provision of a government subsidy for the purchase of new equipment, made a lot of work for these trade associations. The associations also give their members technical advice on the fencing of machinery, fuel utilization, and redeployment.

As may be expected, the central associations tend to deal with matters affecting the county as a whole, the district associations those affecting the locality and individual mills, although there can be some overlap. District associations keep their members informed of agreements on wages and conditions made by the central bodies, on arrangements for local mill holidays, and on local trade statistics. They interest themselves in technical education and training. A human touch, quite in character with the spirit of people in the industry, is shown in one circular sent by a district association to its members a few years ago. It states that a local trade union secretary was about to retire and that permission had been asked for representatives of the operatives to make a collection in the appropriate mills to provide a testimonial to the retiring officer. The circular expressed the view of the chairman of the employers' association 'that members will, on this particular occasion, wish to co-operate in this effort to mark in an adequate manner the services' of the retiring secretary and his hope that members would grant the facility when asked.[1]

The finishing trade associations are organized somewhat differently from those for spinning and weaving. The central body is the Textile Finishing Trades Association which deals with labour and political and commercial matters affecting the whole finishing section of the industry. This is mostly made up, not of district associations, but of a large number (nearly twenty) of associations serving subsections. Some of these such as the Federation of Calico Printers cover a fair

[1] Report of the Bolton Master Cotton Spinners' Association for 1961, p. 77.

range of interests, others such as the Association of Dyers for Rubber Proofing cover fairly narrow specialist interests. These constituent associations mostly concern themselves with the commercial interests of their members. Notably, the Federation of Calico Printers was responsible for the minimum price, production quota, and redundancy schemes that were condemned by the Monopolies and Restrictive Practices Commission in 1954.[1] From January 1968 the sectional associations have ceased to operate as independent bodies and are fully absorbed in the main Association.

The section of the industry concerned with processing cotton waste is served by a single small trade association: the Condenser and Allied Spinners' and Manufacturers' Assocation. There are also other small associations such as the Flannelette Association with largely commercial functions.

The officials of the trade associations carry out the policies laid down by their governing bodies, which are made up of representative employers, but they can, by their advice and by their methods of implementation, strongly affect those policies and their impact. Representative members of any organization, giving only intermittent attention to its affairs, are naturally much influenced by permanent officials who are in daily touch with those affairs. However, officers of the associations tend to work quietly, behind the scenes, in contrast with those of unions who take a more prominent part in developing and publicizing the policies of their organizations.

The main trade associations of the county are affiliated to the International Federation of Cotton and Allied Textile Industries. This was formerly concerned with cotton only, but a few years ago it changed its title to cover also man-made fibres. When Lancashire was the dominant member the headquarters was in Manchester but a few years ago it moved to Zurich—a change that has symbolical as well as administrative significance. Prominent among its activities is the provision of a statistical service.

THE TEXTILE COUNCIL—THE COTTON BOARD

Chapter 1 has mentioned how the industry developed a corporate approach to its problems, and how this found expression in the proposal in the Act of 1939 for the formation of a Cotton Industry Board. This Act was never operated, but during the war a Cotton

[1] See Appendix, p. 159.

Board was formed as a temporary measure. This was successful and in 1948 was reconstituted under the Industrial Organisation and Development Act, 1947. It consisted of people having business interests in the various sections of the industry, trade unionists, and people independent of the industry, under a full-time independent chairman. They were all appointed by the Board of Trade after consultation with industrial organizations and served as individuals who were acceptable to the industry. The Cotton Board was by no means a creature of the government, and came to be accepted as representing, in a broad sense, the industry. It focused industrial opinion, called attention to the industry's problems and difficulties, and acted as a two-way channel of communication with the government. Also, it engaged in a number of activities to further the objectives stated in the general charge: 'to increase efficiency or productivity in the industry, to improve or develop the service that it renders or could render to the community, or to enable it to render such service more economically'. The effectiveness of its work owes much to its permanent staff of about 100 officers.

The increasing use of man-made fibres in the industry affected the activities of the Cotton Board, for example in the coverage of statistics, and at the quinquennial review of 1965–6 it was generally felt that full cognizance should be taken of these developments. Accordingly in January 1967 the Board was enlarged and reconstituted as the Textile Council (for the Man-made Fibre, Cotton and Silk Industries of Great Britain), covering the producers as well as the processers of man-made fibres, and bulking and warp knitting as well as the more typically Lancashire processes described in Chapter 3. The technical links caused by man-made fibres have made it natural to include silk. We may surmise that man-made fibre precedes cotton in the sub-title by design rather than accident, and that the decision must have involved poignant discussion. The wool industry refused an invitation to be included, but there are people who believe that the limitations implied by the sub-title will one day be removed, and that there will be one body serving one textile industry for the country.

The Textile Council has powers to keep a register of firms and to collect a levy. The levy may be up to £625,000; in 1967 the amount collected was £525,000 of which £295,000 constituted a research levy paid to the Shirley Institute.[1]

[1] See pp. 129–60.

The only other compulsory power is to require registered firms to supply statistical information. The Statistical Department issue quarterly statistics of production, employment, machinery in place imports, and exports, all in considerable detail. The Department i very helpful to people (including the present author) who require unpublished information for serious purposes, except of course tha it will not divulge information about any individual firm or that ca be associated with one by inference.

In the early post-war years there was a shortage of labour in the industry and the Recruitment and Training Department of the Cotton Board engaged in propaganda, organized the reception o recruits from Central Europe ('displaced persons'), carried out a Training Within Industry scheme, and encouraged and facilitated the establishment in mills of such amenities as canteens, rest rooms day nurseries, and first-aid rooms.

Later, the subsequently formed Productivity Department introduced new and sophisticated methods for training operatives and developed general courses for foremen, and a range of courses for managers, directors, and trade union officers in work study, management accounting, the costing of re-equipment policies, management 'games', quality control, inter-firm comparisons, and operationa research procedures. Some of these have been 'appreciation' courses extending over only a few days, others have been for people who wil practise the techniques. The Department has an establishment at Didsbury, on the outskirts of Manchester, and this virtually forms a staff college which has had a great effect in introducing modern management practices into the industry. It continues under the Textile Council and its importance is, if anything, enhanced by the establishment of the Training Board under the Industrial Training Act, 1964.

The Cotton Board had two departments aimed at promoting sales of 'Britain's cottons'. The Export Department provided information for merchants and sent missions abroad. The Market Research Department obtained market information and conducted promotional campaigns. The only cogent criticism that was made of these activities was that the money devoted to them was pitiably small and, by modern commercial standards, the effort was puny. Now the Textile Council has an Overseas Trade Department which does much the same things as the former Export Department and prepares cases for submission to government bodies on import and export problems.

The Cotton Board was the mouthpiece of the industry in making repeated representations to the Government for action to limit imports, especially from India, Hong Kong, and Portugal. Under the aegis of the Textile Council this activity has been regularized by the formation of an Imports Commission, which includes representatives of the hosiery and garment-making industries and of retailers, as well as of the industries covered by the Textile Council. At this time (late 1968) the industries can only hope that the Commission will be more effective than the Cotton Board was.

The Colour, Design and Style Centre for the industry, set up in 1940 and continued under the Cotton Board and the Textile Council, is claimed to have been the first such centre to be set up in the country. It aims at promoting high standards of aesthetic design and, through fashion parades and exhibitions, at calling attention to the excellence of the design of British cloths. People who are inclined to criticize British designs should see this centre before coming to conclusions.

The Textile Council has an Education and Information Department which provides a public relations service for the industry and generally performs the functions indicated by its title. It operates a Careers Advisory Service and administers Textile Council scholarship schemes.

In addition to their regular activities, the Cotton Board and Textile Council have from time to time undertaken special tasks. One big job was the administration of the Cotton Industry Act, 1959, for which the Cotton Board, among other things, provided inspectors to ensure that redundant machinery was in fact destroyed, and examined re-equipment schemes to ensure that they complied with the provisions of the Act. In 1967 the Textile Council undertook an elaborate 'productivity study' aimed at assessing the future market prospects for the industry, and examining costs of production and the economic effects of new machinery, long runs, the scale of operation, and multi-shift working. Labour productivity and machine utilization are being studied in a number of mills. One outcome will be suggestions on changes in the structure and management of the industry to meet the conditions of the future.

One activity of the Cotton Board, which is continuing under the Textile Council, has been the organization of conferences. In the early post-war years there was in the industry a strong ferment of ideas and opinion associated with the drive for recruitment and production, and the modernization of mills, machinery, and methods.

Week-end conferences provided a much-appreciated means for exchanging and propagating ideas, and the enthusiasm at some of the very early conferences amounted almost to exaltation. Soon a pattern emerged, with an autumn conference held at Harrogate for discussing broad questions of policy, and a spring 'productivity' conference held at St. Annes or Southport for discussing management technicalities. The Harrogate conferences have varied in the liveliness of the interest shown by the delegates. In the second half of the 1950s, with trade deteriorating, speculation on what the Government would do to help stimulated interest, particularly since cabinet ministers made pronouncements at some of the conferences. Later the industry has become disillusioned and the Harrogate conferences have become mildly interesting routine events. The 'productivity' conferences have not been held for some years.

Plate 42. Houses at Todmorden. The top storeys are reached from the road up the hillside at the back.
Plate 43. A side street in Bolton. The houses are typical of workers' dwellings in the mill towns surrounding Manchester.

CHAPTER 6

Other Organizations

COTTON MARKETS

Cotton is grown in many countries, on small peasant holdings as well as large plantations. It has to be harvested, collected into centres for ginning (i.e., separating the fibre from seed) and baling, and transported to central markets in the growing country and thence to the importing country. In each growing area cotton is harvested at one time of the year, but its use in mills is spread over the year, and the annual fluctuations in the crop do not correspond with those in demand; consequently the crop has to be kept in store for long periods and finance is required for this. These operations involve a complex series of processes—technical, commercial, and financial—which, for the Lancashire spinner, have their outcome largely in the operations of the Liverpool cotton market—or did up to World War II. At that time, this was probably the most important cotton market in the world.[1]

Importers and merchants would hold in Liverpool stocks of many varieties of cotton, large enough to keep the mills going for four or five months, which they would offer for sale, and would also know of other lots available in the country of origin. Some merchants, knowing some of the more stable requirements of spinners would offer their own 'marks' of cotton of recognizable quality, and would select the bales necessary to maintain the quality of the mark over the years. The spinner using this cotton would be dependent on the skill and reliability of the merchant. Many spinners would prefer to appraise the cottons available for themselves and make their own

[1] See J. A. Todd, *The Marketing of Cotton*, Pitman, London, 1934.

Plate 44. A small side road in Littleborough taken from the main road. The side road is unmade and used as a communal yard.
Plate 45. Cottages on a minor road on the outskirts of Littleborough.

I

selections. Cotton quality is complex and appraisal was largely an experienced, subjective assessment, and skill in choosing cottons that would meet his technical requirements was part of the spinner's art. Moreover, there was money to be made by purchasing bargain lots of cotton provided their quality was right.

A spinner has described to me the process of buying cotton. He would have in Liverpool a broker who, as an intermediary between himself and merchants' brokers, would serve his interests. He would telephone to his broker saying broadly what sort of cotton he wanted (the broker's familiarity with his needs would simplify communication) and arrange a day when he could visit and see samples. The broker would assemble in his office suitable samples from a number of merchants and on the appointed day the spinner would visit the office, examine the samples, and make his selection. Then the appropriate merchants' brokers would be called into the office and the spinner would haggle with them over the prices, a merchants' broker having to refer to his principals if the final price offered for a lot was below one he had been authorized to accept. After the price had been agreed, delivery details would be settled and a contract would be signed. The price and description of the cotton would be reported to the Liverpool Cotton Association, and would form part of the data on which the official quotations would be based. The parties to these negotiations would have general market information as well as knowledge of their particular circumstances, and the spinner would find conversation with other spinners in the train between Manchester and Liverpool one good means of adding to that information.

An important part of the market information would be contained in the Weekly Circular and Daily Report of the Liverpool Cotton Association. This would list the prices of transactions, give the extent of business in different cottons and official quotations of nearly 150 different descriptions of cotton. There would also be information on stocks and movements of cotton, prices on other cotton markets, and foreign exchange rates. Most of this information only has meaning if a cotton can be described; if, for example, spinners and merchants know closely what a Mississippi 'strict middling', $1\frac{3}{32}''$, or a Menoufi 'fully good' cotton is like. A very elaborate system of description by staple and type, and of grading (largely according to the cleanliness and colour of the cotton) had been developed. Within each type and grade, however, there was variation in secondary qualities, leaving

imple scope for the exercise of skill in selection and for variation in
price.

The transactions so far described were on the 'spot' market; the
cotton was sometimes referred to as 'spot' cotton, and the officially
quoted prices were 'spot' quotations. In parallel operated the so-
called 'futures' market, an institution for insuring spinners and
traders against part of the losses (and gains) that could arise from
fluctuations in the price of cotton. The main features of this market
as it appears to the spinner will now be described, and for simplifica-
tion we ignore the differences in qualities between cottons.

Suppose that Spinner A has in January bought at the January price
a certain weight of cotton which he expects to spin into yarn and sell
in March at a price corresponding to the March price of cotton. He
will lose money if, between January and March, cotton falls in price,
and gain if it rises. Now suppose that Spinner B has contracted to
supply at some future time an equal weight of yarn for which he
will require to purchase cotton in March, and that the contract is
made in January at a price based on the January price of cotton. If
between January and March cotton changes in price his experience
will be the opposite of that of Spinner A, and if the two spinners can
get together they can off-set their potential gain or loss. If cotton
falls between January and March, Spinner B can make a payment to
Spinner A so that neither gains nor loses, and vice versa if cotton
rises in price. This they, in effect, do through the process of buying
and selling 'futures' cotton. This is done by entering into a 'futures'
contract which is an undertaking to accept or supply cotton at some
stated future time, at a price specified when the contract is entered
into. Spinner A would thus hedge his January purchase of real
cotton by selling March 'futures', and Spinner B would hedge his
sale of yarn by buying March 'futures'. When March came, Spinner
A could honour his contract by supplying the cotton he bought in
January or, if he wanted to use it in his own mill, he could purchase
other cotton on the spot market at the March price and supply that.
In either event, the gain or loss on the futures transaction would
off-set the change in value of the real cotton. Correspondingly,
Spinner B could, in March, accept the 'docket' cotton, as that
delivered under a futures contract was called, and either use it, or
sell it on the spot market and use the proceeds to buy more suitable
cotton. Alternatively, and more conveniently if they could find each
other, the two spinners could exchange matured futures contracts

and make a payment, one to the other, to compensate for the change in the price of cotton. Such is the principle of the futures market; there are many complications in detail, some of which must now be mentioned.

The principle has been presented in terms of a barter transaction between Spinner A and Spinner B, but it is as related to what actually happens as are barter transactions to commerce generally. There were many traders with forward commitments involving cotton: cotton merchants, spinners, cloth manufacturers, and yarn and cloth merchants; and these would constantly be buying and selling futures to hedge their commercial risks. In addition there were professional operators and speculators who would make their living by buying and selling futures. All these traders constituted a very active market, so that Spinners A and B and their like had no difficulty in buying and selling futures, including matured contracts, according to their needs. Normally, the spinner would throughout each trading day keep a running balance of his cotton purchases, yarn sales, and futures contracts, and periodically buy or sell futures to counterbalance any excess of purchases over sales or vice versa—the smallest possible futures contract was for 100 bales or 48,000 pounds of cotton. In such a fluid situation, the choice of the period ahead for the futures was only of secondary importance—at Liverpool it could be for any number of months up to 24 ahead. Traders, as opposed to professional market operators, would try to avoid holding contracts that were close to maturity lest they should be embarrassed by having to handle 'docket' cotton in which they were not interested. Other considerations would be judgement as to the relative prices for the futures for the different months ahead, and how far, generally, the trader felt that he was committed.

Physically, the futures market was a large circular chamber in the Cotton Exchange, with a ringed barrier at which brokers would make their offers to buy and sell by 'public outcry'. The scene is said to have been very lively and at times to have approached pandemonium. According to J. A. Todd,[1] at a busy time there could be as many as one hundred traders shouting offers and making signs of acceptance; many thousands of notional bales of futures cotton could be bought or sold in a few minutes. The quick agreement reached at the ring would, of course, be followed more or less at leisure by a written contract. The chamber was equipped with boards and indicators

[1] Op. cit., p. 63.

giving up-to-the-minute market information, including the direction of the wind! (This was important in the days of sailing ships because it affected the ability of ships to get into Liverpool, and hence the amount of cotton available.) Prices of futures transactions were reported, and official prices were quoted in the Liverpool Cotton Association Circulars. The trader had to deal through a broker who had access to the ring.

Futures contracts were made in terms of particular cottons—middling American cotton was the most important of these—and futures had their own prices for the various months ahead, related to but by no means equal to the current spot price. Futures prices were subject to forces additional to those determining the prices of spot cotton and, moreover, different types and grades of cotton changed in price relative to each other. Consequently the trader concerned with particular cottons, not often middling American, could only partially hedge his trading risks by buying and selling futures; there could be no hedge for changes in the differentials. However, the prices of the cottons of any one important class such as American or Egyptian, and of the corresponding futures, did move broadly together, and the major part of the risk was covered. Certainly, Lancashire spinners relied very heavily on the futures market, and some companies had rules instructing the management to hedge all transactions.

The Liverpool Cotton Association Ltd., which organized the market, provided many facilities besides those mentioned. Forms of contract, rules for transactions, and procedures for the settlement of financial obligations are among the necessities of any market. An important facility was an arbitration service for the settlement of disputes about the quality of particular deliveries not being as good as that of the sample against which the contract was entered into. Defalcations were rare, but differences in technical opinion on the quality of cotton could not be avoided, and the Association's experts provided an authoritative verdict that was respected all over the world.

The Liverpool cotton market has provided an essential service for the Lancashire textile industry. The market has been criticized, sometimes heatedly, but only for the price the industry has had to pay for the service, never (as far as I can discover) for the quality of the service. Speculators, in particular, have been criticized for making fortunes and contributing little, although their function in providing a kind of lubricant to the free activity of the market is recognized.

So far, this description has been of the Liverpool cotton market as it was up to the outbreak of the war. During the war, and for a few years after, the market was closed and cotton was imported an distributed by government agencies. In 1952 private trading in spo cotton was allowed and in 1954 the Liverpool Cotton Associatio reopened the futures market. But if could not revive the former glor of that market. Lancashire uses very much less cotton than it dic and many spinners (especially the combines which are an increasin proportion of the remaining industry) deal directly with shippers in the country of origin. The spot market is thus small, and no spinne can rely on obtaining the cotton he needs at short notice from stock held in Liverpool. The futures market has declined in activity sinc the first year of its revival so that the amount of business done i insignificant in the total of the business of even the reduced industr and people are wondering whether the Liverpool futures marke will survive. The business is no longer conducted on the floor of th Exchange, but in a smaller room. Several reasons are given for the decline.[1] One is that the general movements in cotton prices are no large compared with the relative movements of the different growth that now are used in greater variety than before, so that a future contract is less widely useful as a hedge. Another reason is that cotto prices are subject to the decisions of governments more than to th impersonal forces of the market, and speculators are unwilling t operate under such conditions.

The Manchester Cotton Association was a smaller, paralle organization formed to facilitate the importation of cotton trans ported over the Ship Canal to the port of Manchester, and provide substantially the facilities of a spot market. It is now closed.

YARN AND CLOTH MARKET

The Manchester Royal Exchange was one of the glories of th industry but it continues in operation only until the end of 1968. I provides a convenient meeting-place for spinners, cloth manufac turers, merchant converters, and suppliers of mill equipment. Ther they discuss trade and other politics, arrange business, and talk o the test-match score. The 'floor' of the Exchange is a large hall, with numbered pillars which serve to locate members, and indicator which give market information (Plate 39). 'High change' is on Tues

[1] See B. S. Yamey, 'Cotton futures trading in Liverpool', *Three Banks Review* No. 41, March 1959, p. 21.

day and Friday afternoons, when most members attend; and when the industry was large the floor was crowded and the scene busy. During the war the building was damaged by bombs and subsequently only one half of the floor was reinstated for use as an exchange. Even so, it now never becomes crowded, and activity is quiet, with some 1,200 members moving about seeking others or conversing quietly in small groups. Business is arranged more by telephone and letter than on the floor of the exchange. Plates 38 and 39 contrast the old days with the present and epitomize the history of the industry.

The corporate interests of cloth merchants are looked after by the former Cotton and Rayon Merchants' Association, recently renamed the Textile Converters Association (Cotton, Man-made and Allied Fibres), and a section of the Manchester Chamber of Commerce.

PROFESSIONAL ORGANIZATIONS

The chief professional organization serving the industry is the Textile Institute. It was formed in 1909 to promote the technical and professional interests of all the textile industries of the country—cotton, wool, linen, silk, jute, hosiery, lace, carpets, laundering. It has nearly twenty sections in the main textile districts of the United Kingdom and, in addition, ten or so sections abroad. It is the only fully organized textile professional body in the world and is strengthening its foreign connections, but nevertheless it is primarily a British institution.

The Institute organizes many meetings in the various centres for the discussion of technical topics, larger conferences (some of them abroad), and an annual conference. It sponsors the publication of textbooks and publishes journals which have been the medium for the propagation of much of this century's knowledge of the science and technology of textiles. In co-operation with the British Standards Institution it develops standards on testing methods.

The Textile Institute runs a system of examinations and other tests, as a result of which it awards qualifications of standing. Its qualified members can practise as Chartered Textile Technologists and in that activity are bound by a professional code. It also has a system of honorary awards.

The Textile Institute is by no means exclusive to the Lancashire textile industry, but that industry still provides one important base for its activities, and the Institute is certainly very important for the industry.

The Society of Dyers and Colourists is a smaller and more restricted organization that operates largely as a learned society.

There are in Lancashire nine associations of managers which are joined in the National Federation of Textile Works Managers' Associations. Their main objective is the propagation of technical knowledge, and they mostly hold meetings at which lectures are given and discussions are held; annually the Federation organizes a week-end conference.

In addition to all these bodies, there are in some towns independent textile societies.

TECHNICAL EDUCATION

The University of Manchester Institute of Science and Technology has a textile department which operates as a regular university department, giving instruction according to its own syllabuses, conducting research, and awarding its own degrees.

In addition there are in the county five technical colleges with active textile departments: at Bolton, Blackburn, Burnley (associated with Nelson), Oldham, and Salford. Before the war there were substantial textile departments in other colleges but they have virtually ceased to exist. Even in the five colleges named, the textile departments are not as large as they were, but they are all well staffed and equipped.

The technical colleges hold courses in preparation for examinations by external authorities. The Cheshire and Lancashire Institutes and the City and Guilds of London Institute give certificates for technicians—operatives and foremen who supervise the operation of the machines. There are Ordinary and Higher National Certificates and Diplomas in textiles, and the Associateship of the Textile Institute for technologists and managers. These colleges hold full-day courses which are attended mostly by foreign students, but the most common system is 'part-time day release', whereby the student working in a mill is given leave for one day a week to follow a course, and adds three evenings a week. By following such a course a student can obtain his qualifications in five to seven years from leaving the grammar school. The 'hard way' has not been made easy! The sandwich system favoured in some industries, whereby the student spends one half of the year full-time in the works and one half in the technical college finds no acceptance in the Lancashire textile industry. The old system whereby the student gained all his learning by evening study is disappearing.

The heads of departments in technical colleges expend much time and energy in finding out what the local industries need in the way of courses and in securing the support of employers for courses. They also arrange special groups of advanced lectures and discussions on new developments in technology and management for managers and technologists who are already qualified. They also do what they can to adapt their arrangements to the needs of shift-workers.

Many of the students in the technical colleges come from abroad, some from countries that are Lancashire's strong competitors. This causes grumbling among employers. However, it is advantageous to this country that the technologists in other, especially the emerging, countries should be familiar with British machinery and with British ways of thinking and living; and these students help to support provision for technical education in the county on a scale the local industry alone could not justify or support—a facility that benefits local industry.

The educational facilities provided by the Productivity Department of the Textile Council have been mentioned, and those provided by the Shirley Institute will be mentioned in the next section.

The Cotton and Allied Industries Training Board, set up in July 1966 under the Industrial Training Act, 1964, has powers to collect a levy from the industry and the duty to arrange and pay for courses and other activities for providing technical and managerial training for all grades in the industry and pay the expenses of participation. It published its first Grants Scheme in June 1967.

The technical press also constitutes a valuable educational facility. For most of the period covered by this book there were two commercially run weekly journals and four 'glossy' monthlies; now the weeklies are reduced to one. These report on happenings and technical developments all over the world that are of interest to the Lancashire industry, and reflect the industry's opinion on questions of immediate concern. New machines, and new mechanical and organizational developments in particular mills, are described. Many of the articles on broad technical topics are written by acknowledged authorities and are of high quality.

RESEARCH ORGANIZATIONS

The textile industries are often regarded as old, craft industries, relying entirely on the skill and experience of the people who work in them, and owing little or nothing to science. That they are old cannot be denied, and they owe very much to the skill and experience of their workers; but science also plays an important part in the development of their technology. The new fibres and other materials that proliferate give opportunities for the development of new products and present special processing difficulties. The pressure of competition requires the adoption of ever more efficient machines and processing methods, which require control. Consumers of textiles, especially of textiles such as tyre cords used in other industrial products, require ever closer adherence to specifications and ever more reliable quality. All these developments are too rapid to be met by the slow accumulation of experience which is the way a craftsman learns his job; they require the more rapid and certain accumulation of knowledge that comes from the application of science. In addition, modern science supplies tools that are useful in textile research: X-rays, radioactive isotopes, ultra-highspeed photography, electronics, and electronic computers are among the tools now regularly used in textiles.

The textile industries do not spend as much on scientific research as many industries do. In a survey published by the Department of Scientific and Industrial Research, the expenditure in 1958 on research and development is given, for each of several groups of industries, as a percentage of the value of the net output of that group (net output is the value of the products minus the value of materials used). Textiles is grouped with leather, leather goods, and clothing, and the percentage for the group is 0·9—the same as for iron and steel. The aircraft industry tops the list with a percentage of 35·7 and electronics and precision instruments come next with percentages of about 12. Manufacturers of wood and paper, and printing come bottom with a percentage of 0·25, and food, drink, and tobacco with a percentage of 0·6. The average percentage for all manufacturing industry excluding aircraft is 2·6. Textiles, which is a dominating part of its group, thus comes well down the list. Many people think that these industries should spend more on research and development, but no one has yet thought of a good criterion for deciding how much should be spent. However, the money spent by the Lancashire industry is considerable and the results are very important to the industry.

Some large firms in the Lancashire industry have research departments, some of the products of which have been notable. Examples are the anti-crease resin treatment for cotton, developed in the laboratories of Tootal Broadhurst Lee and Company, which has already been referred to (p. 9), and the polyester fibre known under the trade names of Terylene and Dacron, discovered in the laboratories of the Calico Printers' Association, a combine of primarily printing firms.

Research done in the research departments of companies closely associated with textiles also benefits the industry. The fibre producers not only develop new fibres, but they help the processers (spinners, weavers, and so on) to overcome special difficulties, and they develop end-uses. Dyestuffs and other chemical firms do research on the application of their products to textiles. Textile machinists, notably Textile Machinery Makers Ltd., the large combine that makes spinning machinery, have research departments to facilitate the development of new machines.

The Lancashire industry also benefits from the research and development done abroad. The nylons, acrylic fibres, the bulking of filament yarns of man-made fibres, and some new developments in the resin treatment of cotton have originated largely in the U.S.A., and France, Germany (West and East), and Switzerland have contributed important new developments in textile machines.

The co-operative research organization of the industry is the Cotton, Silk and Man-made Fibres Research Association (C.S.M.F.R.A.), better known as the Shirley Institute. This was formed in 1961 from the amalgamation of the British Cotton Industry Research Association (B.C.I.R.A.) and the British Rayon Research Association (B.R.R.A.).

The B.C.I.R.A. was one of a number of industrial research associations formed shortly after the end of the First World War. At that time a number of industrial leaders were impressed by the technical weakness of British, compared with German, industry because of its slowness to apply science, and they fostered the establishment of associations, financed by firms in an industry and helped by government grants, to do research of value to the industry as a whole. The B.C.I.R.A. was established for the (then) cotton industry of the United Kingdom, and set up its headquarters in the Manchester suburb of Didsbury, naming it the Shirley Institute.

Towards the end of the Second World War the up-and-thrusting rayon industry decided that a research association was necessary for the processers of its fibres (then largely viscose and acetate rayon) and subsidized the establishment, in 1947, and the running of the B.R.R.A. At that time the wisdom of this procedure was questioned by some people in the Lancashire industry because the new fibres were processed by firms in the traditional textile industries: cotton, silk, linen, and the work of the new research association must inevitably overlap with some of that of the older bodies—especially the B.C.I.R.A. The developments in the raw materials utilized by the Lancashire industry had already been recognized in 1927 by the establishment at the B.C.I.R.A. of a rayon department, and a department was added in 1935 to carry on the work of the former British Silk Research Association. However, those in charge of the rayon industry adhered to their view, and the B.R.R.A. was formed. Synthetic fibres came later, and their utilization was the subject of research at both the B.C.I.R.A. and the B.R.R.A. Since the former cotton industry used by far the greatest quantity of man-made fibres, as compared with other textile industries, the B.R.R.A. tended to serve it more than the others, and overlap with the B.C.I.R.A. was greater than with the other textile research associations.

In 1961 the logic of the situation was accepted by all concerned and the two associations were amalgamated. It was convenient and economical to house the new association at the premises of the former B.C.I.R.A., and Shirley Institute was retained as the name of the headquarters.

The annual income of the two research associations had a strong upward trend over the years up to 1960, that of the B.C.I.R.A. increasing even during the depressing years of the 1920s and 1930s. At the amalgamation the combined income dropped and has remained fairly level since then. The industry has felt unable to increase its contributions in line with the general increase in costs, and the situation is being met by some contraction in size and by increasing the amount of money earned for sponsored research and specific services. In 1966–7 the income was a little over £600,000 and the staff was about 380, including about 100 university graduates and professionally qualified people recruited from many universities and many parts of the country.

The governing body is a council, consisting of representatives of the industry, trade unionists, and representatives of the Ministry of Technology. The Council has a number of committees which advise on financial and research policy, and through these about one hundred people from the industry participate in the affairs of the C.S.M.F.R.A., and ensure that its activities are in line with the industry's requirements. The Ministry exerts only a little positive influence, and substantially the Council of the C.S.M.F.R.A. is an autonomous body, responsible only to the members of the Association —i.e., the firms in the industry. The chief executive officer is the full-time Director of Research who, with his staff and acting under the instructions of Council, provides the continuous attention and activity necessary for the formulation and implementation of effective policies.

In addition to laboratories and service departments, there are large workrooms equipped with full-scale and small-scale industrial machinery, so that the research work and development can be carried a long way towards practical application before mill trials are embarked upon.

In spite of pressures for practical results, the Institute has always given a prominent place to basic research—research that is relevant to the industry's interests but is undertaken for the sake of information without any particular application in mind. Such work requires more resources than a university can be expected to devote to one industry, its motivation transcends that of even a large industrial company, which is properly concerned with the company's own products, and so it is a proper field for a co-operative research association. It is necessary as a foundation for new technical developments and for understanding what is happening when new machines and processes are put to work. It enables the industry to deal with the technical problems of the future as well as those of the present, and experience has amply justified the emphasis given to it.

The Institute also does research on more immediate but general practical problems such as those associated with high-speed carding in the spinning mill, the use of electronic clearers in winding, the projection and checking of the shuttle in weaving, and the washing of cloth in finishing. It also undertakes sponsored research and deals with the day-to-day problems of individual mills, notably with diagnosing the causes of defects in cloths, and discovering where in the long chain of processes they occurred.

All this work has naturally produced ideas for new machines and processes, and the Shirley Institute has made contributions to the technical innovations of the past decades, some of which have served their time and have been superseded. Notable devices that are still in use are the automatic sizing referred to in Chapter 3 (p. 70) and the system for extracting dust-laden air from cards referred to in Chapter 4 (pp. 83–4). The Institute has also developed an automatic system for the cardroom in the spinning mill, the commercial value of which has yet to be proved.

I believe, however, that the Institute's main influence has been through the information it has gained and disseminated, helping the industry to overcome the practical difficulties of applying new developments from whatever source and to make the best use of them. For example, in Chapter 3 it is described how important in modern spinning and weaving the precision of machinery is; the work of the Institute has played a large part in discovering that importance and in showing the directions in which precision is required. One outcome has been the development of instruments and methods of control. An example is the Shirley Analyser, an internationally recognized instrument for measuring the amount of waste material in bale cotton. Another, an old one, is in the Fluidity Test for controlling bleaching. If bleaching is too severe the cloth is weakened, even to the point of being made unserviceable, but this test, developed by the Shirley Institute soon after its foundation, enables bleachers to establish conditions for avoiding such damage. The whole list of controls is a very long one.

Work on the products of the industry has resulted in the devising of some new cloths, for example a satisfactory cotton blanket for use especially in hospitals, but its main success has been in the understanding that has been gained of how cloth properties are affected by those of fibres and yarns and by the constructional particulars, and in the development of new instruments for measuring properties.

Of the general departments, that labelled Technical Economy was a pioneering venture when it was formed. From early days the Institute has been interested in the impact of its work on the economics and efficiency of the industry, on management practices, and on the work of the operatives. This activity began in a small way and grew until ultimately it became organized in a separate department. The work of the department included some elaborate studies of labour productivity in spinning, which helped in post-war redeployment activities, and work studies, which helped in the development of new wage systems. One product of the early work was the invention of 'work sampling', which is now a standard work-study technique. Technical economy information has increasingly been used to guide the applied research and development work of the Institute, and to advise the industry on the economic consequences of new technical developments in the textile world at large, and on situations in which their adoption is likely to be profitable.

The effectiveness of the Institute's work has depended on the vigorous steps taken to communicate results and to encourage their practical application. In the early days the staff were mostly scientists unfamiliar with the industry, and it took time for them and the industrialists to get to know and appreciate each other. In the late 1920s a Liaison Department of technologists was formed. These visited the mills, explained the work of the Institute to managers and overlookers, helped to solve mill problems, particularly those arising in applying the results of the Institute's work, and brought back to the staff news of those problems. The scientific staff also visited the mills from time to time and many have built up close personal relationships with managers.

Finished research projects are published openly to the world as scientific papers if they are of general interest, and privately to members if they have immediate practical application. Members of the staff also give lectures. Co-operation is maintained with technical colleges so as to ensure that new knowledge finds its way into their courses.

Although the Institute staff has given considerable direct help by dealing with the day-to-day problems of mills—some would say too much—a healthy situation depends on the mill staffs being able to apply research results for themselves and to take the knowledge into account in their daily work. Consequently, the Institute runs a variety of training courses and conferences, an activity that has been so much increased recently that a training officer has been appointed. The number of people in responsible positions in the industry who have had training at the Institute or are ex-members of its staff must run into hundreds. The Institute is at pains to emphasize that the training it offers is confined largely to 'Shirley' matters and so is complementary to that offered by technical colleges and other organizations rather than overlapping.

Some of the impact of the Institute's work is through the use in the industry of instruments and other equipment devised there. At the beginning the Institute supplied or arranged for the supply of such equipment directly, but the activity grew and in 1953 Shirley Developments Ltd. was established to take it over. This is an autonomous company, separate from but closely linked to the Institute, which arranges for the manufacture and supply of equipment, directly or under licence, attends to the commercial negotiations involved, and encourages sales by the devices used by commercial companies generally. It has also acted as agent in the marketing of devices originating at other research associations. Any profits go to pay for more research.

The Shirley Institute has lively connections with other organizations, within the industry and without, and generally acts as the technical and scientific arm of the industry. Trade organizations and the Factory Inspectorate naturally turn to it for help, and it was specially helpful in the developments in the industry that followed World War II. It and its staff support the work of the Textile Institute and contact with other textile research associations is maintained through a standing committee of their directors. There are many *ad hoc* contacts with government departments. Members of the staff are active in their professional bodies and maintain contact with universities. Over the years they have paid many professional visits abroad. Generally, the Institute serves to bring all the resources of modern science to the industry.

When the Shirley Institute was formed it was one of very few textile research organizations in the world, and it built up an outstanding position. Now, textile research is done in great volume and with great ability in many places and the Institute is no longer unique. Nevertheless it continues to hold a position of high respect in the textile and scientific worlds.

OTHER ORGANIZATIONS

There are a number of organizations which are less intimately part of the industry than those described earlier in this chapter, but which have close connections with it.

Plate 46. Weaving shed in the Rossendale Valley with its associated village of stone-built houses. The sloped roofs of houses up the hillside are typical.
Plate 47. Modern flats in Salford on the site of demolished factories. The Bridgewater Canal is in the foreground.

Prominent among these are the British Cotton Growing Association (B.C.G.A.) and the Cotton Research Corporation (C.R.C.), formerly the Empire Cotton Growing Corporation. Early in this century Lancashire spinners were nervous at their dependence on one source of supply, the U.S.A., for most of their raw material—at that time about four-fifths of imported cotton came from there. The cotton famine resulting from the American Civil War had not been forgotten, and Lancashire was also at later times embarrassed through shortage of supplies. At that time the growth of cotton textile industries in other countries, including the U.S.A., was seen as a threat to the supply of raw materials. The B.C.G.A. was formed on the initiative largely of Lancashire spinners, and in 1904 was incorporated by Royal Charter to encourage the development of cotton growing in the British Empire as it then was. The capital of nearly £½M. was subscribed largely by spinners and workers in Lancashire and was used in the development of new cotton-growing areas, by surveying land, experimenting with varieties to grow, supplying seed, guaranteeing prices to peasant growers, erecting and working ginneries, and providing credits for the marketing of crops. The money was used as far as possible to support and encourage the efforts of others in the areas, and to build up enterprises that would be commercially self-supporting. The activities of the B.C.G.A. were not the same in each area, and depended on the local needs; it is in West Africa that the Association has taken most initiative and where its activities have been most comprehensive and decisive.

Although intended to be run as a self-supporting commercial organization, the B.C.G.A. expected to make losses at the beginning, and the prospectus stated that no dividends would be paid for seven years. These expectations were realized up to the First World War. In 1914 J. A. Hutton, then Chairman of the Council of the B.C.G.A., remarked that wherever the Association worked successfully it carried prosperity with it, adding, perhaps somewhat ruefully, 'though it frequently happens that the Association itself is the only body which derives no profit from its transactions'.[1] Gradually

[1] *The Work of the British Cotton Growing Association*, June 1914, p. 10. Published by the B.C.G.A.

Plate 48. A mill cheek by jowl with dwelling houses in Bolton.
Plate 49. The small works of a commission warp sizer in a side lane in Todmorden. There is a pile of empty beams to the right. The corner of the building to the left of the lane has been chamfered to widen the lane. The whole is a set-up that has 'jes' growed' and has been there for a very long time. Photo taken in 1958.

K

financial returns began to be received and now the B.C.G.A. is reasonably profitable company whose shares can occasionally b bought.

The B.C.G.A. worked closely with government departments from the beginning. As cotton growing became established and govern ment became more organized in the territories, the B.C.G.A. tende to recede into the background. Now, most of the territories ar independent countries and the Association has only the status of an ordinary trading company.

After the First World War cotton growing in the Empire had no developed far enough to relieve anxiety over the supply of cotton t Lancashire, and it was felt that further efforts beyond the scope an resources of the B.C.G.A. were needed. As a result of a Governmen report in 1920 (Cmd. 523), the Empire Cotton Growing Corporatio was established under Royal Charter, which was amended in 196 when the title was changed to Cotton Research Corporation. I received a capital grant from the Government at the outset, and fo some years it received payments from the Lancashire industry. Sinc the last war the value of its work has increasingly been recognized b the governments of the growing countries, and they now make sub stantial financial contributions. The C.R.C. is not a profit-making body.

The C.R.C. engages in the scientific work needed for the develop ment of cotton crops, and most of its fifty or so officers are gene ticists, entomologists, plant physiologists, plant pathologists, and s on. These officers breed varieties of cotton that give good yields o satisfactory cotton, they study the control of pests and cotton diseases, and they develop suitable methods of cultivation. The Corporation has a research station at Namulonge in Uganda, nea Kampala, (which is likely to be transferred to the Uganda Govern ment in the future) and it has staff working on government research stations in several African countries. In these countries the C.R.C. works closely with the government agricultural department. So far, these fruitful relationships and co-operative activities have survived the political changes that have occurred in Africa, and indeed the C.R.C. officers have helped the countries over some of the difficulties that accompany the changes in agricultural conditions. There is no sign of the Corporation reducing its activities.

The C.R.C., like the B.C.G.A., was started on account of the interests of Lancashire, but always the benefit to the growing countries from the development of cotton crops has been a strong consideration. Now the second consideration is paramount, but the Lancashire origins of the C.R.C. have not been obliterated, and there are many Lancashire people on the Council and Executive Committee.

The work of the B.C.G.A. and the C.R.C. has succeeded abundantly. The U.S.A. is still an important source of medium-staple cotton, but it no longer has a virtual monopoly. The benefit from this extended supply is shared by cotton spinners in all countries, for Lancashire has no priority or preferential terms when buying cotton. These developments in cotton growing result from the efforts of many people and organizations, but the contribution of the B.C.G.A. and C.R.C. has been enormous.

The benefits to the growing countries have been considerable. Cotton is a major contributor to the national wealth of Sudan, Nigeria, Uganda, and Tanzania, and a substantial contributor in other African countries; and again the influence of the B.C.G.A. and the C.R.C. has been important. It is significant that newly independent countries in Africa are glad to associate themselves with the work of the C.R.C. The work of the B.C.G.A. and the C.R.C. is among the creditable activities of the British people—and the British credit is due to Lancashire!

At school we were taught to think of the cotton industry when thinking of the horrors of the industrial revolution, and of the factory acts as being designed to improve conditions in cotton mills. The Factory Inspectorate of the Ministry of Labour, which supervises the application of these acts, is not an organization of the Lancashire textile industry—the factory inspector of an area is not confined to the factories of any one industry. Nevertheless, the Inspectorate is an important part of the Lancashire industrial scene.

In past years—up to the 1920s and in places even later—the factory inspector was regarded as the natural enemy of the manager, for it is his job to see that the regulations under the act are complied with and to prosecute for infringements. If an inspector visited a mill, the manager would warn his friends over the telephone that he was 'about'; and I have heard from inspectors stories of subterfuges they would adopt to get into mills without warning so as to detect infringements which would be covered up if the manager had only a few minutes' warning.

Now all that is changed. Competition for labour and the dictates of conscience have produced in managements a desire to provide good conditions in the mills, and the factory inspectors are accepted as making a positive contribution to that end. They advise individual managements on things in particular mills, and on committees with the trade unions and trade associations co-operate in working out recommendations on lighting, spacing of machinery, ventilation, and so on, for general application. There is a standing Health and Welfare Committee of the industry, set up by the (then) Ministry of Labour with the Senior Inspector as Chairman. The zeal of factory inspectors may sometimes outrun that of managers, but the activities of the inspectorate are generally accepted as a welcome part of the industry's facilities.

There are technical facilities that are not run by the industry, but are available to it and are much used. The Manchester Chamber of Commerce has a Testing House which performs officially recognized tests on textile materials, such as are required in commercial transactions. Firms also make much use of consultants to advise on special problems, particularly in management.

CHAPTER 7

The County

The Lancashire textile industry is so closely associated with the county and adjacent districts that no portrait would be complete without some indication of the geographical and social background.

First, the county is important to the industry, for most of the processing of cotton and the related processing of man-made fibres that is done in the U.K. is done there. Thus, the Textile Council records that of 87,000 looms in the U.K. running on cotton or man-made fibre fabrics in 1967, 78,000 or 90 per cent were in Lancashire. No corresponding figures are given for spinning but the percentage is probably higher since there are weaving mills in Macclesfield and East Anglia that have changed from silk to man-made fibres, whose looms are included in the 87,000. There is no information for finishing but the Lancashire share is undoubtedly large. The substantial outposts of the industry in the Glasgow area and Northern Ireland have also suffered a decline so that Lancashire's predominance in the U.K. remains.

Secondly, Lancashire has depended very heavily on its textiles. Even as late as 1954 the percentage of all insured workers engaged in textiles in several typical textile towns such as Blackburn, Bolton, Burnley, and Oldham was about 30. In Nelson it was 50, and in Royton 69 (76 for females alone). As textiles has declined and other industries have developed, this dependence has decreased. In 1966 the percentage of workers in textiles was between 8 and 12 in Blackburn, Bolton, Burnley, and Oldham; in Nelson it was 24 and in Royton 40. But however low the percentage, the memory of the industry remains strong.

This recollection is helped by the way in which mills, especially spinning mills, dominate much of the scene. The fact that many of them are now occupied by other industries does not alter their appearance and there are many places in industrial Lancashire where one can from a hill see over a large area and note the many chimneys and mills (Plate 40). Mr. Geoffrey Moorhouse records that from a

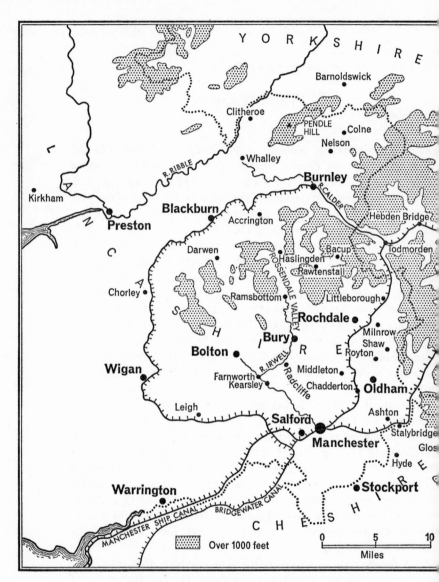

THE LANCASHIRE TEXTILE AREA

hill-top above Bury and Bolton he once counted 127 chimneys. Further, in spite of much rebuilding, the towns and villages show most of the features that they developed with the industry. Also, the people are the same, and many, if not most, even if they do not work in the industry, have parents and other relatives who have done so. The special links of the county with the industry are weakening but they are yet strong.

TOPOGRAPHY—THE MANCHESTER CONURBATION

Manchester (638,000 inhabitants) is the metropolis of the industry. Here are the Royal Exchange, the offices of most of the industry's organizations, the merchant houses, and the head offices of many of the producing firms. There are also textile factories within the city boundaries. For the Lancastrian it is a place to be visited on business or perhaps for an occasional shopping spree, a theatre show or concert, or a trip to Belle Vue—and then left. Manchester will not be described here.

Separated from Manchester by only the River Irwell is the independent city of Salford (148,000), the scene of Walter Greenwood's *Love on the Dole*, the film version of Stanley Houghton's *Hobson's Choice*, and the television programme of the 1960s *Coronation Street*. Its importance as a textile centre has declined drastically. The deep-water docks that constitute the Port of Manchester are in Salford. The city has not been very impressive to the eye, having few public buildings, no large shops, no city centre, and much slum property. But all that is changing. Slums and disused factories are being demolished and tall blocks of flats are being built (Plate 47). New public buildings are being erected in an area around the old Art Gallery so that that is becoming a centre for the city. Prominent among these are the buildings of the new Salford University which, with its halls of residence and playing fields, will contribute materially to the visual amenities of the city. The former Manchester Racecourse, contained in a bend of the River Irwell, provides a fine site for some of these developments. With Manchester so near, Salford seems unlikely to develop a substantial shopping centre.

Almost encircling Manchester and Salford is an inner ring of county boroughs with strong textile interests, spreading over an arc from Wigan (78,000) to the west, through Bolton (158,000), Bury

(63,000), Rochdale (86,000), and Oldham (111,000), which is north-east, to Stockport (142,000) to the south-east, which is just in Cheshire. To these may be added as part of the circle the municipal boroughs of Ashton-under-Lyne (49,000) and Hyde (38,000), also in Cheshire. These towns are between seven and eleven miles from Manchester, except that Wigan is about twenty miles away. Within this circle are about twenty municipal boroughs and urban districts with textile interests, of which Leigh (46,000) will be the subject of further mention. The whole constitutes the Manchester conurbation.

Wigan is and has always been as much a mining as a textile town, possibly even more so, and so has suffered from the effects of decline in two industries. Bolton is one of Lancashire's more spacious and prosperous towns. It is proud to number among its sons Samuel Crompton, the inventor of the mule, whose sixteenth-century half-timbered house, Hall i' th' Wood, is a museum. The first Lord Leverhulme started his career in the Bolton area. Bury is noted for its connection with Sir Robert Peel, and for its black puddings. Rochdale remembers that John Bright was once a prominent citizen—the textile firm of John Bright and Brothers Ltd. still flourishes there—and that Richard Cobden was once its Member of Parliament. Here, too, Gracie Fields worked as a winder in a spinning mill and discovered the talent that made her Lancashire's own music-hall singer. The first Cooperative shop in the world was in Toad Lane and the local society is the Rochdale Equitable Pioneers Society.

Oldham, Ashton, and Hyde are near to the high Pennines and beyond them are only a few small textile towns and villages extending a little way into the valleys. Stalybridge (22,000) and Mossley (10,000) are the most important of these. Glossop (17,000), in Derbyshire at the foot of the Snake Pass, has no spinning or weaving remaining, but there is some finishing. Beyond Stockport, in Cheshire, is Bollington (5,000). This had some large spinning mills where the finest (i.e., thinnest) yarns in the world were spun, but the mills are all closed or put to other uses.

In the sector of the circle between Rochdale and Oldham are the spinning areas of Royton (16,000) and Shaw (or Crompton, 14,000).

Plate 50 (facing, above). Victoria Square and Town Hall, Bolton.
Plate 51 (facing, below). The Roman Catholic church of St. Raphael at Stalybridge.
Plate 52 (over, above). Blackburn market on Whit Monday, 1964. The market hall with tower is now demolished. In the background to the left is the town hall.
Plate 53 (over, below). A tripe stall in the Blackburn market of 1964.

Plate 54 (*over*, *above*).The Le[
and Liverpool Canal at Bla[
burn. It is no longer in use a[
the lock-gates and barges [
rotting. In the middle of [
background is a roofless dere[
mill.

Plate 55 (*over*, *below*). Ever[
supporters at the Cup semi-fi[
match between Everton a[
Manchester United in 19[
played on the ground of Bol[
Wanderers.

Plate 56 (*above*). The walk [
the Congregational Sund[
school at Radcliffe in 1967.

Plate 57 (*left*). Part of [
'Golden Mile' at Blackpo[
Many queer things are to [
seen in the sideshows to [
right, in addition to the m[
orthodox features of a seas[
resort. To the left is the pro[
enade skirting the beach.

The Manchester conurbation is mostly on a plain, with slight eminences here and there, and broken by an occasional steep-sided valley, notably that of the River Irwell. The main roads pass through built-up areas, and the traveller sees mostly houses and factories. In places the industrial and housing development has been untidy, and there are derelict areas of land left unused. The Irwell Valley between Bolton and Manchester is specially depressing, and the river itself is polluted almost beyond redemption. In places, electrical power stations dominate the scene (Plate 41).

Between the towns, the housing runs often in a thin line and behind there is land that is still used for farming. Towards Rochdale the near-by hills become prominent. In the Wigan direction urbanization is less intense and agriculture becomes more noticeable. Characteristics of the landscape around Wigan are coal mines, derelict 'tips' of mining spoil, and 'flashes', which are lakes left by former mining operations and now much used for sailing. In these districts and around Bolton, land subsidence due to the collapse of old underground workings is an ever-present hazard to property.

Until the middle inter-war years there were tramways almost everywhere, some of them very rough and hazardous to other traffic, but these have gone. Most of the roads were formerly paved with stone setts. When the alternative was a water-bound surface these were presumably very durable, particularly with horse-drawn lorries with iron tyres, and were good for horses pulling heavy loads up steep hills. Now they have been superseded, but setts continued to be used for the left-hand side of roads going up-hill for a long time.

TOPOGRAPHY—OUTER AREAS

About thirty miles from Manchester in a general northerly direction is an outer arc of large towns which almost mark the limits of the main textile area. Preston (109,000) and Blackburn (103,000) are slightly west of north and may be regarded as being beyond Bolton. Accrington (41,000) and Burnley (79,000), almost due north, are beyond Bury, and Todmorden (17,000) is north-east and beyond Rochdale.

Preston was the home of Horrockses (now defunct as a manufacturing unit) as well as many other textile concerns. Even in the heyday of textiles, however, other industries were of comparable, perhaps greater, importance. Among other things it has flourishing docks, being at the head of the estuary of the Ribble, and the Dick Kerr works of the English Electric Company, which makes heavy electrical gear and aircraft (the ill-fated TR2 aircraft was made there). It is the centre of much of the county administration. Every twenty years, except when wars intervene, the town holds a festival known as the Preston Guild. For many Lancashire people Preston's significance is that it is the gateway to the Fylde district, with Blackpool and Fleetwood, and to North Lancashire and the Lake District. Being at the lowest point at which the Ribble can be crossed it is a bottle-neck for traffic—or was until M6 was made.

Preston is on the plain but the other towns are in hilly country. Thus, one can stand at vantage-points and see over large parts of Blackburn and Burnley, with their concentrations of factories and their streets of houses running up the hillsides. Todmorden is just over the border in Yorkshire but is postally in Lancashire and is essentially a Lancashire textile town. At the junction of three narrow valleys, it is built partly on very steep slopes (Plates 29 and 49), and is surrounded by rugged steep cliffs and hills. One local feature is that some houses built into the hillside are four stories high and are in effect two houses, one over the other. The lower house is reached from a road at the front and the upper one from a road up the hillside at the back (Plate 42). Todmorden is associated with the Fielden family (pp. 17 and 149); it is also the home town of the late Sir John Cockcroft, who was a director of his family firm of textile manufacturers as well as a very distinguished scientist.

Further from Manchester than this outer arc of towns are a few outposts of the Lancashire textile industry. Beyond Preston there are mills at Kirkham, on the Fylde, and at Lancaster. North-east of Blackburn, in the Ribble Valley, is Clitheroe (13,000), which still has some weaving, but is also the market town of a substantial agricultural district, as becomes very apparent on market days. Roughly north-east of Burnley are the important textile towns of Nelson (31,000) and Colne (19,000). Colne is about six miles from Burnley and the intervening road is entirely built up. North of Nelson, in Yorkshire and remote on the moors, is the weaving town of Barnoldswick (10,000), pronounced 'Barlick'. An outpost, well inside Yorkshire to the north-east of Todmorden, is Hebden Bridge (5,000).

Between the outer and inner arcs of large towns are several smaller towns of textile significance. Chorley (31,000) is on the plain, and Darwen (29,000), under a shoulder of the high moors, is contiguous with Blackburn. In or near the Rossendale Valley (Plates 31 and 46), which runs north from Bury, are Ramsbottom (14,000), Rawtenstall (23,000), and Haslingden (14,000). Bacup (17,000), between Rochdale and Burnley, is surrounded by moors. Littleborough (11,000) is between Rochdale and Todmorden.

There are also many villages, most of which have, or have had, a textile mill or works. Their names—Withnell, Crawshawbooth, Oswaldtwistle, Milnrow, and so on—are part of the essence of Lancashire.

The towns in this area between the outer arc and the inner circle are more widely separated than those within the circle, and the countryside is more apparent. Most of the area consists of high moorland, much of it rising to over 1,500 feet, cut by valleys, broad and narrow. There is not much colour on the moors, the vegetation being at best a dirty green and the rocks and stone walls being nearly black. On a foggy day, or after snow has lain on them for a few days, they are forbidding rather than drab. But the outlines of the hills are grand and the scenery is often dramatic, particularly when backed by some of the cloud formations that are common. The valleys in the moorland area are softer and greener, but still somewhat bleak. From many points there are views over the valleys, but no extensive vistas.

To the west and north, the land falls to the plain, and from the high ground there are extensive views towards the sea and the hills of the Lake District. Here the atmosphere becomes cleaner and the vegetation lush. A prominent feature of north-east Lancashire which almost overshadows Burnley and Nelson, is Pendle Hill, a ridge about five miles long which rises to about 1,800 feet.

The Ribble Valley, beyond Pendle and on the edge of the textile area, is outstandingly green and beautiful. At Whalley, between Blackburn and Clitheroe, are the ruins of a thirteenth-century abbey in a secluded spot on the banks of the River Calder, a tributary of the Ribble, and apparently as remote from industry as is any place in the country.

INDUSTRIES

There is a strong tendency in Lancashire for different districts to specialize in different branches of textile production. Thus, most of the fine spinning from Egyptian types of cotton is done in and around

Bolton and Leigh, medium spinning from American types around Oldham, and coarse spinning also from American types around Rochdale. In weaving, Rochdale tends to produce heavy cloths for industrial uses. Burnley, Nelson, and Colne have only a little spinning. Burnley was formerly noted for its weaving of plain medium-weight cloths known as 'Burnley printers', but trade in these qualities of cloth has been specially vulnerable to competition from low-cost imports, and the reduced industry of Burnley now produces a wide range of cloths including a little printer cloth. Nelson has been known for its fine cloths, especially for fine two-fold poplins in their heyday, and provided a good nursery for the weaving of filament rayon when it first appeared. Nelson is exceptional in having an unusually high proportion of men weavers, power-loom weaving being normally a woman's job. Colne specializes in the weaving of coloured cloths. Preston and district, and Clitheroe also, weave light cloths of high quality from fine yarns. Blackburn lost its special line when the dhoti trade collapsed in the 1920s and has had to make a wide range of goods. Todmorden spins and weaves for the production of drills, and Hebden Bridge weaves corduroys and fustians. The Rossendale Valley is noted for its sheets and flannelette blankets made from waste cotton (as well as for its slipper manufacture). All these specializations are tendencies rather than rigid lines of demarcation, and doubtless they are being weakened by present-day commercial pressures.

With the decline of the textile industry, other industries that have been in the county for a long time have expanded and new ones have come in. A detailed and up-to-date survey of the industries of Lancashire is given in the book *Lancashire, Cheshire and the Isle of Man*, mentioned at the end of this chapter. Here it is enough to say that important industries include: engineering, both heavy and light; man-made fibre production; the manufacture of heavy and light electrical equipment, radio components, motor cars and lorries and buses, aircraft, garments, leather, and boots and shoes; and the administration of mail-order businesses.

TOWNSCAPES

Although parts of the Lancashire textile districts are in rural surroundings, some being in glorious country, the urban and industrial scene predominates. It is less depressing in the more isolated towns with the country 'on the doorstep'. Some of the streets of dwellings, particularly in the larger towns, are slums or almost so; some are neat and are brightened by fresh paint on the woodwork and 'donkey stone' on the doorsteps and window sills (Plate 43). (The rag-and-bone men, who used to supply the donkey stone, now find it hard to come by and some of them offer firewood instead.) Some people show their pride in their houses by turning the windows into imitation leaded lights and by polishing painted steps, gate posts, and wall tops. Some of the side streets are really communal yards (Plate 44). On the outskirts of the smaller towns and villages the older houses take the character of country cottages (Plate 45). In the Manchester conurbation the houses are mostly of brick, built to a standard pattern; in the fringe areas towards the Pennines stone is used and windows are mullioned. In some of the older houses in the Rochdale–Todmorden area windows in the top storey form long rows—Plate 45 would show something of the effect if the windows that have apparently been blocked out by stone were replaced. Hand-loom weaving was once done in lofts lit by such windows, and accessible by outside stair-cases, and it is likely that this has influenced the style of building even where it is not directly responsible for the fenestration. Where a terrace of houses follows the slope of a hillside, as often happens, the roof is also sloped to follow the gradient, presumably for cheapness in construction (Plate 46).

Most of the houses were built well before World War I, but there are also estates of houses built between the two wars (Plate 29), and since World War II. Some slum clearance is in progress, property is being modernized, and there are proposals for improving the environment. *The Deeplish Study* (H.M.S.O., 1966) shows that there are great possibilities in these directions for the Deeplish district of Rochdale. Salford is the first town to build tall blocks of flats for housing (Plate 47).

Traditionally, workers have lived near the mills (Plates 46 and 48), and it is only in recent decades that motor transport has made it feasible, and local shortages and surpluses of labour have made it necessary, for them to travel to work. Some mills run buses for distances of about twenty miles in order to transport their workers. Mills are not often very close to the centres of the larger towns, but sometimes they are on a main street. Sometimes a small works will be tucked away in a side lane (Plate 49).

In addition to houses for the workers there are the estates of detached and semi-detached houses for people of other economic classes, each house with its garden, and architecturally these are neither better nor worse than similar houses in all parts of the country. There are also large mansions, formerly occupied by successful mill-owners, and now often used by some large firm or public body as an office or hostel or museum or something of the sort, or divided into flats. Most of these estates and mansions are a little away from the town and industrial centres. Most of the larger towns have one or more streets or squares of seemly Victorian houses, presumably the former homes of well-to-do business and professional people, and now the offices of solicitors and the like.

The shopping centres of the larger towns are almost indistinguishable from those in other parts of the country since many, if not most, of the shops belong to the national chains. However, typical Lancashire names such as Clegg, Haworth, Platt, Whatmough, and Winterbottom, are to be seen over some shops. The smaller towns and villages are still largely served by local shopkeepers, and in the larger towns there are 'around the corner' shops owned by local people. Many of these shops are constructed by having a shop window put into a dwelling-house.

The public buildings mostly reflect the architectural ideas of late Victorian and Edwardian times, although there are some modern buildings, most of which are schools and colleges. A few of the towns have a spacious town centre. Preston has one, dominated by the Harris Library, an imposing structure surmounting steps which set it off. Bolton's centre is dominated by its town hall (Plate 50) a classical building with a later addition. Rochdale has an outstanding town hall, the cornerstone of which was laid by John Bright in 1866. It is justly described in the town guide as 'a rich example of gothic architecture', the emphasis being on the word 'rich'. The effect, both outside and inside, is impressive and pleasing, and the surroundings are spacious and, except in one direction, worthy. Most towns are now undergoing the considerable building developments that are to be seen all over the country.

Some of the churches are left over from mediaeval Lancashire, but most churches and chapels are products of the nineteenth and early twentieth centuries. A rather gaunt Gothic seems to have been favoured for churches; St. George's, Stockport, is exceptionally attractive, being a Pugin church. There has been some modern building of churches, some of it, especially that of the Catholics, being quite adventurous (Plate 51). Lancashire has always been a stronghold of Unitarianism and a notable church of this denomination is that built at Todmorden by the Fielden brothers. This was described in a nineteenth-century publication as

a gothic building of exquisite proportions, having a beautiful spire one hundred and ninety-six feet in height, and containing, inside and out, much decoration of a chaste and costly character. In the interior various coloured marbles have been used with splendid effect, and the chancel window and the rose window over the principal entrance are triumphs of the stained-glass worker's art, the chancel window being especially beautiful, with its series of illustrations of the chief incidents in the life of Christ. A peal of bells, a carillon, and a large organ are the musical features of this noble edifice, which was built at a cost of £36,000. An inscription on the floor of the principal entrance records the fact that the church was erected by Samuel, John, and Joshua Fielden.

Mostly the Nonconformist chapels have an undistinguished architecture the effect of which is made almost grim by the patina of soot that covers almost all buildings of any age.

The market in the smaller towns is usually an open space on which stalls are erected on market days. In the larger towns such a space surrounds a building in which there are stalls open on several days in the week. Most of the goods to be bought in a market are the same as those in the shops but prices tend to be somewhat lower, except that nowadays the supermarkets also offer some goods at low prices. The market is a good place for out-of-the-way things such as fents or remnants of cloth, odd pieces of leather, and pottery of second quality. Locally produced cheeses, poultry, plants, and so on can be purchased from stalls run by the producers. Plates 52 and 53 were taken in Blackburn market as it was in 1964. It is now demolished and a new one has been built in another part of the town. This is architecturally modern and very ordinary, and at least to some of the older people it is functionally unattractive, although it is doubtless efficient.

If some local patriot were to state that the best parks in Lancashire towns are as good as the best in other towns of comparable size in the country, his claim would be hard to confute. Some of these are extensive estates that formerly belonged to landed gentry. A notable example is Towneley Park at Burnley which, with its seventeenth/eighteenth-century hall, belonged to a family of that name whose connection with the district extended over seven centuries. The hall is a municipal museum and art gallery.

Lancashire has several canals which have provided water for industry as well as transport. Mostly these are now mouldering (Plate 54). The Bridgewater Canal (Plate 47), which skirts the south of Manchester, is still in action, and the Manchester Ship Canal brings cargoes of cotton as well as other things into Manchester.

The traveller's impressions of an area depend a good deal on the weather and atmosphere. Generally the atmosphere is smoky. The smoke of years has blackened the buildings, and the current haze prevents good clear views. Its only virtue is that it sometimes gives good sunsets. Smoke is becoming less as factories have turned to electricity for power, and as homes are using smokeless fuels, but it has by no means been eliminated from the scene. On a wet or snowy day everything looks specially dreary, and South Lancashire has much of this sort of weather. A hot fine day, on the other hand, seems almost to accentuate the prevailing drabness. Only a fresh spring day or a crisp autumn day can really conquer the environment. Writers about the scene seem to be mostly people unto whom the lines are fallen in pleasant places, even if some of them have originated in the area, and on these the impact of the squalor of Victorian and Edwardian industrialism is almost overwhelming. Such graces as the towns display, the parks and gardens, and the more agreeable suburbs give relief but are apt to be overlooked.

THE WAY OF LIFE

It may be thought that life in the drab surroundings of industrial Lancashire would be nasty and brutish, if not short. Mr. Walter Greenwood, from the experiences of his early life in Salford, paints in his books a picture of the sordidness of working-class life there before World War II and passionately condemns the conditions that gave rise to it—it is to be hoped that improvements in the social services and in economic conditions have removed at least some of the worst features portrayed. George Orwell creates a similar impression in *The Road to Wigan Pier*. Two or three years ago I read a newspaper article about the intense and frustrated desire of a young couple to escape from the sordidness of life in the Gorton district of Manchester. At the best, housewives find it hard to keep their homes and curtains clean in the murky surroundings. *The Deeplish Study* describes the attitude of people to their environment in that slum-like area, and there are many criticisms of such things as dirt, untidiness, raffic noise, and inadequate facilities for children to play. There is plenty of evidence of the seamy side of life in the textile towns.

But this is not the whole story. The districts referred to are not the whole of industrial Lancashire, and dispirited slum-dwellers do not constitute the whole population. Further, most people who live in any district in any part of the country or world come to terms with it —they have to—and achieve a satisfying life. Lancashire people have a deep affection for their home district, and be it never so squalid, 'there's no place like home'. Many people even liked living in Deepish and were appreciative of the social life, which is perhaps more important for human beings than the physical environment. Some years ago I used to visit a parson friend in Farnworth, and in particular remember going for a walk with the family along the banks of a derelict canal in perfect contentment. I also attended church functions at which a palpitating social life was evident, to say nothing of the religious life.

A close study of social life and its changes in Leigh has been made by Dr. W. Watson of the Department of Social Anthropology and Sociology, Manchester University, and he presents some results in an article in the magazine *Discovery* (May 1963). Until the last few decades Leigh depended largely on coal-mining, cotton textiles, and engineering, and mostly the enterprises were either owned by local people or run by people with strong local attachments, who contributed to the life of the town, and many of whom provided leadership. Now coal-mining and textiles have declined, and the ownership of remaining enterprises has changed—coal-mining is nationalized, and textile mills and engineering works have become attached to large corporations. The consequence is that 'the resident population is in the main "working class", with a minority of shop-keepers and professional persons, such as parsons and doctors who service them. Managers and officials on a higher level tend to live outside the community. . . .' The possibility the motor car gives these people 'on a higher level' of working in Leigh and living in some delectable rural place has doubtless contributed to this development. A consequence is that the social leadership formerly given by the industrial leaders has been largely lost. In spite of this a strong community spirit and local pride survives in Leigh, sustained by a continuity of residence of the working people (almost two-thirds of the adult population were born and bred there and most of the remainder have moved in from neighbouring places) and by the activities of churches and

L

chapels, political clubs, and sports clubs. The leadership given by local trade union leaders, already mentioned in Chapter 5, remains

The open domestic fire must have done much to make life bearable It makes the home a cheerful refuge from the outside gloom even while adding to that gloom when smoky coal is used as a fuel.

The quality of life is also enriched by the urban amenities that ar provided generously in Lancashire as in other parts of the country The professional theatre of J. B. Priestley's *Good Companions* i dead, but amateur theatricals flourish, and besides Manchester a least Bolton and Oldham have repertory theatres. The cinema now seems to need the support of bingo. For music-lovers there is th Hallé Orchestra which plays often in Manchester and occasionall in the surrounding towns. All towns have concerts—Bolton i particular often advertises chamber concerts by first-rate players Choral societies are very popular.

The usual public bowling greens, tennis courts, football grounds and swimming baths are commonplace, and there is at least one public golf course municipally owned. Football is popular in Lan cashire, as in most heavily populated parts of the country (Plate 55) as the motorist discovers if he tries to drive near a football groune when the match is just over. Besides Manchester City and Mancheste United, Burnley is in the first division, and Blackburn Rovers Preston North End, and Bolton Wanderers are in the second. Rugb is played in the Northern 'Rugby League' version as well as 'Rugb Union'. It is part of the folklore that players in the Lancashire Cricke League (support for which is declining) take cricket very seriousl and play for victory, with none of the nonsense of playing for th game. Rivalries are said to be keen, especially between Lancashir and Yorkshire. I once saw part of the annual match between the tw counties at Old Trafford, but was more struck by the decorum ir the expensive seats and the mountains of litter in the popular part than by any intensity of feeling displayed. Admittedly the battin was very slow. However, Mr. Graham Turner gives a more authentic picture of Lancashire (and Yorkshire) cricket in *North Country*.

Outside the Manchester conurbation at least, good country i never far away, and many people enjoy walking in the Pennines cycling, and fishing—especially from canal banks. The moderr practice of going for rides in motor cars produces, on a fine Sunday traffic congestion in the Preston–Blackpool area enough to satisfy the most gregarious.

One Lancashire custom is the Whitsun 'walk' in which the children of the Sunday-schools in their best clothes parade through the town with banners flying, usually behind a brass band (Plate 56). On a hot sunny day only the perspiring bandsmen in their uniforms and parsons in their black clothes look uncomfortable; on a wet day the affair must be a test of endurance for all. These walks are under attack from people who object to the interference with traffic.

Another feature is the 'wakes week' (now fortnight), when substantially all the factories in a town close so that the people take their holidays all at the same time. Different towns take their holidays at different times spread over about three months according to a timetable. Some people stay at home and some go away, but the life of the town takes on a special muted quality during the period. Now, many of the workers go to other parts of this country or abroad for their holidays, but Blackpool continues to be very popular. It is reasonable to suppose that this was built and developed to cater for Lancashire textile workers, and their robust taste for flamboyant entertainment is doubtless responsible for its character—its South Shore funfair, its Tower and ballroom, and the sideshows of its 'Golden Mile' (Plate 57 . One poignant feature of wakes week is the respite it gives to harassed mill managers in times of bad trade, giving new orders for products a chance to catch up with production.

Lancashire has several special items of food. Lancashire hot-pot consists of mutton chops and perhaps sliced carrots in a casserole, with a covering of potatoes; hot-pot suppers are part of the social scene. The meat-and-potato pie, based on beef, is popular as a dinner dish for factory workers and is to be purchased from the 'shop around the corner'; it has the attraction that by reducing the proportion of beef the price can be kept low. Tripe, cow-heel, and pig's trotters are to be bought in market-places (Plate 53) and from U.C.P. (United Cattle Products) shops. Black-puddings, associated specially with Bury, are basically suet, ox- or pig-blood, and oatmeal contained in a kind of sausage-skin and boiled. Genuine Lancashire cheese, not the nondescript substance so often sold as such, has a characteristic and, to some people, agreeable 'bite'; one variety is sold as 'Leigh toaster'.

The way Lancashire people speak is fairly familiar, at least to those who listen to Lancashire comedians. To southerners it is indistinguishable from the Yorkshire way, but the discerning can detect variations even within Lancashire. Characteristics of the accent

L*

are the broad *a*, and the pronunciation of the *u* in butcher as other people pronounce the *o* in love, and vice versa. Characteristics of the forms of speech are the clipping of the definitive article (*th' mill* for *the mill*); the use of *luv* as a general form of friendly address; the occasional use, especially by older people, of such dialect words as *gradely* (worthy, estimable) and *thrang* (busy); the accepted grammatical solecism; and the exclamation *'ee*. ''Ee, I were reet glad to see 'im; 'e were a gradely lad' is the sort of sentence that can be heard.

Lancashire people are sometimes thought to be droll and outspoken, also somewhat slow-witted but astute. People of these sorts are doubtless to be met, but perhaps comedians have created an exaggerated impression of those as general characteristics. The people are also thought to be friendly and warm-hearted. I have found them to be so, but so also have I found people in other parts of the country. The people of Lancashire of course vary, as do those in any other county. A distinct way of speaking is apt to create the impression of a distinct general character and quite ordinary statements made in an unfamiliar accent seem to have a special impact; but it would require a deep and extensive investigation to discover for different parts of the country whether such distinctions of character are real and if so how strong they are.

FURTHER READING

This chapter is based on impressions gained from moving about the county and industry for about forty years, from associating with some of its people, and from some reading. The picture is far from complete. The complete picture is very complex and any one writer can only present a part of it, from one point of view derived from an experience that is necessarily very limited; for example, the encounters a writer has when passing through a district tend to be with extrovert types of people and, unless care is exercised, he is apt to create the impression that the population is made up of extroverts. It is only by much reading that any approach to a comprehensive picture can be built up. Of the many books on Lancashire the following are some that are relevant to the theme of this one.

Lancashire, Cheshire and the Isle of Man by T. W. Freeman, H. B. Rogers, and R. H. Kinvig (Nelson, London, 1966) is a considerable academic study of the geology, demography, and economics of the region, which gives good space to the textile industry.

North Country Bred by C. Stella Davies (Routledge & Kegan Paul, London, 1963) is a family history which portrays working-class life, mostly in the Manchester area, and covers a good period until about World War II.

Lancashire by Walter Greenwood (Hale, London, 1951), besides surveying the whole county, has vivid descriptions of life and the scene in the textile districts, especially in Salford. The whole is seen through strongly tinted spectacles, although it would be hard to specify the tint.

North Country by Graham Turner (Eyre & Spottiswoode, London, 1967) is partly about Lancashire. It is mostly based on interviews and observations recently made during visits to a few towns.

Britain Revisited by Tom Harrisson (Gollancz, London, 1961) includes several chapters on life in Bolton and one on Blackpool. It is based on a Mass Observation survey made in 1960 and notes changes that have occurred since a previous survey in 1937.

Britain in the Sixties: the Other England by Geoffrey Moorhouse (Penguin Books, Harmondsworth, 1964) has a chapter on Lancashire. The book may almost be regarded as a sequel to J. B. Priestley's *English Journey* published in the 1930s.

Works of imagination that picture the county and its life include novels and plays by Walter Greenwood and stories by T. Thompson. The plays *Hindle Wakes* by Stanley Houghton and *Hobson's Choice* by Harold Brighouse are almost classics.

APPENDIX

Reports on the Industry since 1930

GENERAL REPORTS ON THE STATE OF THE INDUSTRY

Committee (of the Economic Advisory Council) on the Cotton Industry, (Cmd. 3615). Pp. 31. H.M.S.O., London, 1930.

This is the 'Clynes Report' of a Government committee of five people, none of them belonging to the industry. It is based on evidence received from representatives of most of the bodies in the industry. After analysing the causes of the loss in trade, the report reaches the conclusion that the only salvation lies in a reduction in the costs of production. 'Lancashire must choose. She can lose her trade, she can reduce her standard of wage and living, or, perhaps, she can keep her trade and her wage standard by reducing costs and improving methods.' The industry is castigated in the following terms: ' . . . we are satisfied, from the evidence laid before us, that the British cotton industry has failed to adapt its organization and methods to changed conditions and so has failed, and is failing to secure that cheapness of production and efficiency in marketing which alone sells staple goods in the East today.'

There follows a discussion of the organization of the industry into its sections, of possibilities for technical improvement, and of the need for improving the links between processes and between production and marketing, the last being in order to secure the benefits of long runs. The recommendations were under the headings of technical improvements, amalgamations, and the development of co-operative effort throughout the industry.

Although the national interest in the well-being of the industry was recognized, the problems were for Lancashire to solve by her own actions, Government action being regarded as a last resort.

Report on the British Cotton Industry. Pp. 147. Political and Economic Planning (P.E.P.), London, 1934.

This report by anonymous authors is based on a survey of the experiences of the industry after World War I. The changes in trade, especially the losses in exports, are analysed in some statistical detail and causes are identified. There are also detailed descriptions of: the organization of the industry into sections and of the markets; schemes that had been tried for eliminating redundancy of machines and for organizing sales co-operatively; the various amalgamations that had taken place, and their financial background; technical developments; and the cotton industries of some other countries.

Recommendations are presented in the form of ideals to be aimed at rather than as cut-and-dried schemes, but they are well elaborated. They cover such items as: dealing with price-cutting; amalgamations (vertical amalgamation is not favoured); the setting up of a Marketing Corporation; improvement of co-operation between cotton ginners and spinners; countering Japanese competition by concentrating more and more on the production of speciality and 'fine' goods; making it possible for India to import more Lancashire goods by increasing the consumption in Lancashire of Indian cotton; the enforcement of agreements between the organized employers and operatives on wages and labour arrangements. Progress towards the ideals is seen to require a strong 'Industry Council' and improved statistical and other factual information, and the existing Joint Committee of Cotton Trade Organisations is mentioned as a possible basis.

Lancashire and the Future: the present position and prospects of the cotton industry. Pp. 29. Joint Committee of Cotton Trade Organisations, Manchester, 1937.

This is a short, factually supported, and discreetly worded polemic emanating from the industry, and chiefly concerned with the effects of the Government's commercial and industrial policies on the cotton industry's exports. The various tariff arrangements, including the Ottawa Agreements of 1932, are shown to have had little beneficial effect on the cotton industry, and the various subsidies and other 'safeguarding' arrangements to assist agriculture, coal, shipping, steel, and dyestuffs are held to have had deleterious effects in increasing Lancashire's costs and in reducing the capacity of Lancashire's customers to import. While the need for the industry to reorganize itself is recognized, attention is called to the likely effects of the Government's future policies in these directions.

Report of the Legislative Council on ways and means of improving the economic stability of the Cotton Textile Industry. Pp. 167. United Textile Factory Workers' Association, Rochdale, 1943.

Most of this report is factual, being descriptive of the industry in most aspects and its recent history. Special attention is paid to wages and working conditions. There are recommendations for the near future, and a scheme of ultimate socialization of the industry, by placing it under the control of a General Board for the Cotton Industry with strong powers, is proposed.

Report of the Cotton Board Committee to enquire into Post-War Problems. Pp. 55. Cotton Board, Manchester, 1944.

This committee was convened by the wartime Cotton Board and consisted of twenty-eight representatives of employers and operatives, so that the report can be taken as representing the mind of the industry at the time.

The main topic is the steps to be taken by the Government and the industrial organizations to re-establish the industry after the war, and the headings are: organization, the size of the industry and problems of excess capacity, raw cotton supply, re-equipment, the labour force, research, deconcentration, taxation, price management, distribution, and the terms and conditions of international trade. It is emphasized that, in view of uncertainties about the future, particularly about the size of future demand, plans should be elastic. In the well-elaborated statistical part calculations are based on three estimates of the long-term future demand, and at this time it is interesting to note that the most pessimistic of these would require a labour force of 259,000 in spinning, doubling, and weaving (there were 100,000 employed in 1967).

Cotton: a Working Policy, by a Fabian Research Group. Pp. 21. Fabian
    Publications (in association with Gollancz), London, 1945.

A short pamphlet which discusses Lancashire's future in much the same terms as other surveys. One proposal is that redundant machinery should be eliminated by the compulsory purchase and liquidation of firms, rather than by the elimination of machines alone. Price control would then be necessary only to prevent prices from rising too high. The discussion of import policy is concerned largely with the importation of raw cotton. State agencies, which are envisaged as working with private firms, are proposed for helping exports. The whole discussion is more about the principles underlying the various problems and remedies than about precise recommendations.

Cotton: Working Party Report. Pp. 278. H.M.S.O., London, 1946.

The Cotton Working Party was one of many working parties set up by the Government in the early years following World War II to study closely the problems of British industries and make recommendations. This one consisted of four employers and four trade unionists from the industry, and three independent members (a professor of chemistry, a professor of economics, and a management expert), all under an independent chairman —Sir George Schuster. The party did not rely on evidence from witnesses but conducted their own researches, and were assisted by sub-committees covering costs, machinery and plant, and research. The report is comprehensive, covering raw materials and products, industrial organization, equipment, labour organization and management, and research and development. The recommendations include suggestions for compulsory amalgamations, and schemes for eliminating redundant machinery and re-equipment financed by a levy on the industry. Most of the employers and of the independent members dissented from these, advocating a more private-enterprise approach to the problems. The trade unionists made clear their opposition to the dissenters. There were thirty-four recommendations and, in spite of the controversy over some of them, as a whole they had a strong influence on later developments. For a time the report was almost a Bible of the industry.

Plan for Cotton. Pp. 48. United Factory Workers' Association, 1957.

This analyses the situation of the industry and takes account of many previous reports and writings. Cognizance is taken of the imports into the U.K. of cloth from India and Hong Kong, and among the recommendations is a proposal for a Government Imports Commission to control such imports. The Plan was formally abandoned by the Association in 1967 as no longer having relevance.

SECTIONAL REPORTS

Report of the Monopolies and Restrictive Practices Commission on the Process of Calico Printing. Pp. 128. H.M.S.O., London, 1954.

The Commission, constituted of people from outside the industry, had the duty of saying whether calico printing was operated under conditions of monopoly, as defined in the Monopolies and Restrictive Practices (Inquiry and Control) Act, 1948, and if so whether any of the conditions were against the public interest.

The report gives a brief history of the cotton industry and of calico printing in particular, for the latter paying attention to the development of combines and the trade association. The trade association, the Federation of Calico Printers, was formed in 1949, and the Commission was mostly interested in its scheme for minimum prices to be charged for printing and its Percentage Quantum Scheme, both of which covered 98 per cent of the cloth printed in the U.K. According to the latter scheme each firm in the industry was allocated a 'quantum'—a share of the total turnover of the industry estimated from past experience. If in any month a firm exceeded its quantum in the business it did, it paid a sum equal to 20 per cent of the value of the excess into a pool; if it did not reach the quantum it received 20 per cent of the deficit from the pool. One firm could sell its quantum to another, provided it transferred an appropriate quantity of machinery, or destroyed it, at the same time. Then, it was said by the Federation, if a specialist printer suffered a temporary fall in demand for his particular services he would not be tempted to undercut other printers of other lines; and on the other hand no printer would be tempted to expand his trade unduly by undercutting others. The scheme was regarded as a necessary support for the scheme for minimum prices which, in turn, was thought to be necessary to maintain the financial health of firms in times of declining trade and excess capacity. The report also describes a redundancy scheme and other schemes for regulating the industry. There is a chapter on the Calico Printers' Association, the combine which, at the time, had about one-half of the industry's business.

The Commission states:

We have been impressed by the sincerity and strength of feeling shown by the calico printers in defending their arrangements, and by their almost passionate conviction that it is only by such means that a decent living can be ensured for those employed in the industry, its plant maintained and improved, and an adequate supply of new recruits attracted as managers and operatives.

Nevertheless it held, without much concrete evidence in support, that the arrangements must tend to increase prices in the long run and were contrary to the interests of other sections of the cotton industry and the public. It substantially recommended their abandonment.

'The restrictive practices court and cotton spinning', by Alister Sutherland, *The Journal of Industrial Economics*, 8, 1959, pp. 58–79.

Under the Restrictive Trade Practices Act, 1956, the rules of the Yarn Spinners' Association were brought before the Court in 1958 for a declaration on whether they were contrary to the public interest. The case was a big one—it occupied twenty-eight days and written evidence filled 800 files of documents which made a pile 33 feet high—and is reported in the Law Reports. This paper gives a good and well-documented summary, and discusses the legal and economic implications of the issues raised.

The Association was formed in 1949, and was very effective in ensuring minimum prices for yarn. These were held by the Association to have public advantage in preserving processing capacity during periods of temporary recession so that revived demand could be met; in encouraging firms to modernize their equipment and so to produce cheaper and better yarn; in discouraging firms in times of bad trade from producing unaccustomed yarns for which they were not well adapted; in encouraging spinners to concentrate their competitive efforts on giving good quality and service; and in contributing towards the stability of prices through slumps and booms. The Court agreed that these ends were desirable, but found that the Association's activities did not contribute to them materially—certainly not enough to outweigh the public detriment resulting from the loss of a free market. It found, with some doubts, that the abolition of the Association's rules, by accelerating the rate of contraction of the industry, might cause a serious increase in unemployment locally but that on balance the general good to be expected from abolition, especially in its effects on exports, outweighed the detriment.

The Court declared that the Association's rules were contrary to the public interest, but actions by the Association in submission to this view rendered further official action unnecessary.

ACTS OF PARLIAMENT AND RELATED PAPERS

Cotton Manufacturing Industry (Temporary Provisions) Act, 1934

Provided that if the principal employers' and operatives' organizations requested the legal enforcement of a wage agreement, the Minister could, after a public inquiry, make an Order giving effect to this. The operation of the Act was limited to weaving mills in the Lancashire textile area, and in time it was limited to three years in the first instance, although the Act was renewed in subsequent years.

Cotton Spinning Industry Act, 1936

Provided for the formation of a Spindles Board, supported by a financial levy on the spinning industry, with powers to purchase and destroy redundant spinning machinery. The activities of the Board were limited both in time and in the amount of machinery that could be eliminated.

Cotton Industry (Reorganisation) Act, 1939

Provided for the formation of a Cotton Industry Board with specified Committees, with powers to collect money, operate redundancy and price schemes, encourage exports, collect and publish statistics, and provide other services for the benefit of the industry. There was to be a Rayon Committee. In the main it was an enabling Act, requiring subsequent Orders to make it effective.

Cotton Spinning Industry (Re-equipment Subsidy) Act, 1948

Provided for re-equipment schemes for spinning mills to be subsidized to the extent of one-quarter of the cost. An important limitation was to combines of no fewer than three mills, so organized that production could be concentrated in the most efficient of these; and only schemes covering some of the mills of a combine were to be eligible.

Cotton Industry Act, 1959, and subsequent orders

Provided for the organization and administration by the Cotton Board of redundancy schemes, two-thirds of the cost to be paid by the Government and one-third by levies on the sections of the industry. Among the provisos were: that any scheme shall be agreeable to a majority of the section of the industry and that the arrangements shall include compensation for any consequent loss of employment. There was a limitation on the time for which any scheme could operate, but not on the amount of money to be paid.

The Act also provided for Government grants to firms in aid of approved re-equipment schemes, proposed and completed before certain dates, the grants to amount to one-quarter of the cost. There was no limitation on the total grant to be paid to the industry.

Assistance to the Cotton Industry, being the Fourth Report from the Estimates Committee of the House of Commons for the session 1961–62. Pp. 166. H.M.S.O., London, 1962.

This examines the working and effects of the Cotton Industry Act, 1959.

For the redundancy schemes of the Act, the Cotton Board offered to compensate firms for scrapping machinery and placed the compensation at such a level that there would be sufficient voluntary acceptance to reduce the industry's equipment by the desirable amount. This involved making somewhat speculative estimates. In the event, percentage reductions achieved were:

in spinning		48
in doubling		34
in weaving		38
in cloth finishing	bleaching	17
	dyeing	24
	printing	18
in yarn processing		26

These reductions were regarded by the witnesses from the industry as satisfactory. They would have occurred ultimately without the Act, but there was thought to be an advantage that they had been accelerated. The cost of the operation to the Government was about £M12.

At the time of the Report applications for the re-equipment subsidy covered equipment of about £M43 in value, the Government's share of the cost being about £M11. These figures were stated to indicate a rate of re-equipment not very different from what would have been normally expected without the Act, and many of the Committee's questions to the industrialists who gave evidence were directed towards discovering why the subsidy had had such disappointingly little effect. The difficulty of arranging multi-shift working, so necessary to make modern expensive machinery economic, was given as one factor. Owing to the effects of taxation the 25 per cent subsidy was not as attractive as at first sight it seemed. The continued high importation of low-cost textiles from India and Hong Kong weakened the confidence of the industry in its future. Several witnesses drew attention to the weakness of Lancashire's arrangements for marketing its products.

Industrial witnesses quoted ten years as the useful life of new machinery, the term being set by obsolescence rather than physical deterioration.

WAGE ARRANGEMENTS

The Cotton Spinning Industry: Report of a Commission set up to review the Wage Arrangements and Methods of Organisation of Work, and to make Recommendations. Pp. 51. H.M.S.O., London, 1945.
— *Supplement, Mule-Spinners' Wages.* Pp. 20, H.M.S.O., London, 1946.
Memorandum of Agreement between the Federation of Master Cotton Spinners' Associations, Limited, and the Amalgamated Association of Card, Blowing Room Operatives, relating to Wages and Conditions in Cotton Rooms, Blowing Rooms, Card Rooms and Ring Rooms. To be known as 'The Aronson Card and Ring Room Agreement, 1947'. Pp. 30. Federation of Master Cotton Spinners' Associations, Limited, Manchester, 1947.
Cotton Manufacturing Commission: Reports of an Inquiry into Wages Arrangements and Methods of Organisation of Work in the Cotton Manufacturing Industry.
    Interim Report, on weavers' wages and work. Pp. 63. H.M.S.O., London, 1948.
    Final Report, Part I, on weavers' wages and work. Pp. 24, H.M.S.O., London, 1949.
    Final Report, Parts II, III and IV, on wages and work of miscellaneous classes of weaver and other operatives, and on recruitment and training. Pp. 24. H.M.S.O., London, 1949.

These are the reports described in Chapter 4, pp. 101–3. They were often referred to under the names of the chairmen of the commissions: Mr.

Justice Evershed of the spinning commission, Mr. V. R. Aronson of the cardroom negotiating body, and Mr. R. Moelwyn Hughes of the manufacturing commission—all lawyers. Only people closely associated with the working of these bodies can assess the personal contributions of the various people involved, but I know enough of the working of the Cotton Manufacturing Commission to state confidently that the very successful outcome of its work owed much to the drive and leadership of its chairman.

All the reports describe the existing arrangements in the industry and their historical development, and discuss their effects on productivity and efficiency. The revised arrangements recommended are presented in terms of general principles and also in considerable detail, so that little further development was required to produce operating schemes. The *Interim Report* of the Cotton Manufacturing Commission is notable for having what is probably the most succinct paragraph ever to appear in a Government report: '59. The Uniform List must go.' The two reports on weavers' wages are also notable in presenting the results of a considerable amount of experimental investigation. These provided a basis for the recommendations and a test of the likely effects of their application. The whole exercise was an early example of operational research applied on the scale of an industry.

WORKING CONDITIONS

Reports of the Joint Advisory Committee of the Cotton Industry. Ministry of Labour and National Service. H.M.S.O., London, various dates.
Sanitary accommodation, washing facilities, accommodation for clothing, medical and welfare services, decoration and vacuum cleaning. Pp. 9. 1946.
Ventilation, temperature, use of steam in humidification, and lighting. Pp. 16. 1947.
First report on spacing of machinery: cotton weaving. Pp. 12. 1947.
Mule spinners' cancer and automatic wiping-down motions. Pp. 8. 1945.
Mule spinners' cancer. Pp. 9. 1952.
Dust in card rooms. Pp. 9. 1946; Pp. 54. 1952; Pp. 30. 1957; Pp. 18. 1960; Pp. 26. 1961.

These reports present recommendations on the various working conditions in Lancashire mills, as agreed by representatives of the employers, workers, and the factory inspectorate. The list of titles showing the subjects of concern is probably of more general interest than the actual recommendations.

The reports on dust in cardrooms show how solutions to that intractable problem have developed and present the results of many investigations. The climax comes in the 1957 report, where the committee was able to recommend that a device was available which enabled the section of the Factories Act, 1937, requiring a clean working atmosphere, to be observed.

PRODUCTIVITY

Report of the Cotton Textile Mission to the United States of America.
Pp. 76. H.M.S.O., London, 1944.

This is the Platt Report that has been referred to in most post-war reports
on the industry. Statistical productivity studies, notably those of the late
Dr. L. Rostas, had shown that production per man hour was much higher
in the U.S.A. than in the U.K. in many industries (ratios of more than 2 to 1
were common) and this created the general view that the U.K. problems
of supply could be much alleviated and industrial efficiency improved by
studying, and in some degree adopting, American industrial practices.
The Platt Mission visited the U.S.A. to explore this idea for the cotton
industry. Detailed comparative studies for typical mills in the two countries confirm the higher productivity in the U.S.A., and the technical and
organizational causes are analysed. The recommendations for change in
the U.K. are along the general lines followed in subsequent years.

Cotton Spinning
Cotton Yarn Doubling
Cotton Weaving
The British Cotton Industry

Anglo-American Council on Productivity (now British Productivity
Council), London, 1950 and 1952.

The Anglo-American Council on Productivity was formed in 1948 to
promote the economic well-being of the two countries by the exchange of
information on industrial organization and technology. One of its chief
activities was the sponsoring of visits to the U.S.A. of teams of investigation from British industries. Each team of about a dozen people consisted
of managers, technologists, foremen, and operatives. The first three of
the above reports give a full account of conditions in the U.S. industry.
That for cotton spinning has detailed statistical comparisons of productivity in mills in the two countries. The fourth report is that of a U.S. team
that visited Lancashire in 1952.

Index